BUCKS COUNTY
& THE
DELAWARE RIVER VALLEY
ALIVE!

Shari Mycek

HUNTER

Hunter Publishing, Inc.
130 Campus Drive
Edison, NJ 08818-7816
☎ 732-225-1900 / 800-255-0343 / Fax 732-417-1744
Web site: www.hunterpublishing.com
E-mail: comments@hunterpublishing.com

IN CANADA
Ulysses Travel Publications
4176 Saint-Denis
Montreal, Québec H2W 2M5 Canada
☎ 514-843-9882, Ext. 2232 / Fax 514-843-9448

IN THE UK
Windsor Books International
The Boundary, Wheatley Road
Garsington, Oxford OX44 9EJ England
☎ 01865-361122 / Fax 01865-361133

ISBN 1-58843-260-2
© 2002 Hunter Publishing, Inc.

Maps by Toni Wheeler, © 2002 Hunter Publishing, Inc.

Index by Kathy Barber

4 3 2 1

About the Author

Shari Mycek moved to the Delaware River Valley in the mid-1980s, where she launched her freelance writing career. Now specializing in travel, her work has appeared in *Condé Nast Traveler*; *Travel + Leisure*; *The Robb Report*; *Spa magazine*; *Epicurean Traveler*; *The Dallas Morning News*; *The Christian Science Monitor*; *Spirit Airlines* inflight magazine; *Bride's*; *Victoria Magazine*; and *The New York Post*, among others.

About the Alive Guides

Reliable, detailed and personally researched by knowledgeable authors, the *Alive!* series was founded by Harriet and Arnold Greenberg.

This accomplished travel-writing team also operates a renowned bookstore, **The Complete Traveller**, at 199 Madison Avenue in New York City.

We Love to Get Mail

This book has been carefully researched to bring you current, accurate information. But no place is unchanging. We welcome your comments for future editions. Please write us at *Alive Guides*, c/o Hunter Publishing, 130 Campus Drive, Edison, NJ 08818, or e-mail your comments to comments@hunterpublishing.com. Due to the volume of mail we receive, we regret that we cannot personally reply to each letter or message, but your comments are greatly appreciated and will be read.

Acknowledgments

During my daughter's fifth-grade year, her teacher, Jay Glassman, stressed to students that if they can discover something new in their own backyards, they are real travelers. His words stayed with me while writing this guide. Although I have lived in the Delaware River Valley for more than a decade, I was constantly amazed at the scope and talent of the many artists, chefs, designers and creative people living and working in the region. Special thanks to those who graciously invited me into their studios, restaurants and living rooms.

Thank you to my husband, Greg, for his constant support and patience, and to my friend Chris for sharing several Bucks County treasures. A heartfelt thank you to publisher Michael Hunter and editor Lissa Dailey who kept me on track in the writing of my first guidebook.

www.hunterpublishing.com

Hunter's full range of travel guides to all corners of the globe is featured on our exciting Web site. You'll find guidebooks to suit every type of traveler, no matter what their budget, lifestyle, or idea of fun. Full descriptions are given for each book, along with reviewers' comments and a cover image. Books may be purchased on-line using a credit card via our secure transaction system. All on-line orders receive a 20% discount.

Alive! guides featured include: *Antigua, Barbuda, St. Kitts & Nevis*; *Aruba, Bonaire & Curaçao*; *Atlanta*; *Baltimore & The Chesapeake Bay*; *Bermuda*; *Bucks County & The Delaware River Valley; Buenos Aires & The Best of Argentina*; *Cancún & Cozumel*; *The Catskills*; *The Cayman Islands*; *Dallas & Fort Worth*; *Dominica & St. Lucia*; *Hollywood & The Best of Los Angeles*; *Jamaica*; *Martinique & Guadeloupe*; *Martinique, Guadeloupe, Dominica & St. Lucia; Miami & The Florida Keys*; *Nassau & The Best of the Bahamas; St. Martin & St. Barts*; and *Venezuela*.

Check out our *Adventure Guides*, a series aimed at the independent traveler who enjoys outdoor activities (rafting, hiking, biking, skiing, canoeing, etc.). All books in this signature series cover places to stay and eat, sightseeing, in-town attractions, transportation and more!

Hunter's *Romantic Weekends* series offers myriad things to do for couples of all ages and lifestyles. Quaint places to stay and restaurants where the ambiance will take your breath away are included, along with fun activities that you and your partner will remember forever.

Contents

Maps

Dedication

To my own artist, Abby, whose song continuously inspires me.

Introduction

I decided on a region where the landscapes are var-
ied, where farm and industry lived side by side,
where the sea was near at hand, mountains not far
away, and city and countryside were not enemies.

            – Pearl S. Buck

*L*ong before the Broadway "smart set" – Oscar
Hammerstein II, George S. Kaufman and Moss
Hart – "discovered" Bucks County, Pennsylvania in
the 1920s and 1930s, the region surrounding the
Delaware River (in both Pennsylvania and New Jersey) served as a sanctuary for intellectuals, artisans
and Bohemians. Located midway between New York
City and Philadelphia, the region was an easy draw
for artists and actors eager to escape their harried
city lives for a more peaceful countryside existence.

Today, the region's artistic legend continues with intimate cooking schools run by master French chefs,
vineyards and brew pubs, foreign cinemas, theater,
antiques and flea markets, shad fishing on the Delaware, hot-air ballooning and romantic inns.

Sadly, many of these artistic and cultural treasures
go undiscovered by visitors. Those in the area only a
few days (or sometimes just hours) will see the tourist shops and try a restaurant, but ultimately miss
the true artistic essence and spirit of the region.

Bucks County
is home to 12
covered
bridges, all
built between
1832 and
1874.

This book provides an artistic guide to the area and,
most importantly, "connects" the region for visitors.
While many guidebooks refer to Bucks County, Pennsylvania and Hunterdon County, New Jersey, and
the nearby towns of Doylestown and Princeton, they

rarely do so in the same breath (never mind book). Yet, to those living and working in southeastern Pennsylvania and central New Jersey, there are no clear distinctions between counties or states. Bucks County residents often work in Princeton or travel there for shopping or theater (the McCarter Theatre is one of the top regional equity theaters in the country). Those living in Princeton frequently seek out the Delaware River towns – with their cozy inns and tucked-away restaurants – for evenings out and even weekends away.

Like many Delaware River Valley residents, I landed here serendipitously. But over time, the region has become home, and while there are more "McMansions" (massive, executive-style homes) than I ever hoped to see being built on pastoral farmlands, the region remains rich in cultural and artistic treasures. This guidebook reveals many of them.

 # How To Use This Book

Bucks County & The Delaware River Valley Alive! divides the region into six key sections, with the Delaware River serving as centerpiece.

Area Overview

The "tour" begins with the art colony of **New Hope, Pennsylvania**, located on the west bank of the Delaware River in southeastern Pennsylvania. Although it has only four main streets, this tiny town is, itself, a "destination." But your trip just begins here.

Bucks County
& The Delaware River Valley

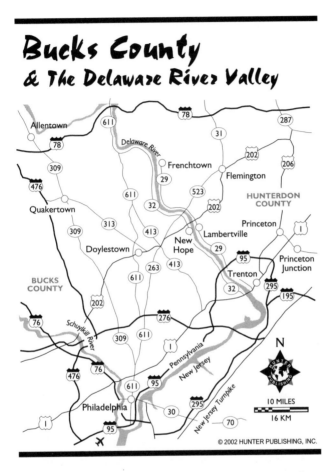

© 2002 HUNTER PUBLISHING, INC.

Part of the allure of any trip to New Hope is exploring, at a snail's pace, the narrow and twisting **River Road** (Route 32), with its charming stone houses, inns and towpath. You'll need a car for this scenic tour, which begins in New Hope and heads north along River Road, with stop-offs in the towns of **Lumberville**, **Point Pleasant** and **Erwinna**.

An iron bridge for both cars and pedestrians connects New Hope, Pennsylvania to **Lambertville, New Jersey**, on the east side of the Delaware.

Lambertville is known as the "Antiques Capital of New Jersey."

While not as scenic as Route 32 (its Pennsylvania counterpart), **Route 29**, which follows the Delaware River on the New Jersey side, is also worthy of exploration. This excursion starts in Lambertville and heads north to **Stockton**, detours to **Rosemont** and **Sergeantsville**, and resumes on Route 29 to **Frenchtown**.

*Don't miss Doylestown's **James A. Michener**, **Mercer**, **Fonthill**, and **Moravian Pottery & Tile Works** museums.*

No visitor to the Delaware River Valley should miss the region's cultural centers: **Doylestown, Pennsylvania**, a half-hour west of New Hope; and **Princeton, New Jersey**, located just a half-hour east of Lambertville.

Princeton highlights include tours of **Princeton University**, the Tony-award-winning **McCarter Theatre**, upscale shopping and stunning architecture.

Geology & Geography

The Delaware is everywhere a river on the brink, holding off extinction, awaiting discovery.

        – Bruce Stutz, Pennsylvania author

The **Delaware River** is the longest free-flowing river on the east coast. Originating in the Catskill Mountains of New York, the river flows a total of 375 miles to the Atlantic Ocean, winding its way through four states – New York, New Jersey, Pennsylvania and Delaware.

In Bucks County and Hunterdon County, the geographic elements of the river are striking. Near Erwinna, Pennsylvania and Frenchtown, New Jersey, the Delaware is narrow and isolated, except for a few islands and bridges, as it twists beneath hillsides and cliffs of strange-colored layers of rocks; in New Hope, Pennsylvania and Lambertville, New Jersey, the river is wider and lazier.

Towpaths and canals flank both sides of the river and tiny islands occasionally part the river in the middle.

The Environment

River Life

Shad run the Delaware River each April, using the non-tidal waters as an opportunity to spawn. **Herring** and **striped bass** follow.

The shad share a long history with the Delaware. In 1896, a record 19 million pounds of shad were caught in the river and Delaware Bay but, about 40 years ago, the Delaware River was so polluted that there was no catch at all. Successful cleanup efforts by the New Jersey Fish, Game and Wildlife Division brought the shad back; in 1982 the first catch was nearly 4,000. Today, Lambertville continues to celebrate the return of the shad with an annual and quite lavish end-of-April **Shad Festival** (see page 18).

The Canals

The **Delaware Canal** in Pennsylvania, and the **Delaware & Raritan Canal** in New Jersey both run adjacent to the river. The canals were built over a period of several years in the early 1800s to move coal from mine to market. Soon after the railroad put the mule-drawn barges out of business, the Commonwealth of Pennsylvania purchased 40 miles of canal and, later, added the remaining 20 miles.

In 1974, the New Jersey side of the canal was designated a state park, administered by the Delaware & Raritan Canal Commission. In 1989, the Pennsylvania side was deemed the **Delaware Canal State Park** and, in 1990, became part of the National Trail System.

Today, the canals and towpaths on both sides of the Delaware are used for recreational walking, hiking, jogging, biking, fishing, birding, canoeing and even horseback riding.

Disappearing Farmlands

During the late 1940s, Bucks County was 67% farmland, with farms occupying over 260,000 acres. As of the late 1990s, the percentage of farmland had been reduced to only 18% of the county, representing 70,000 acres. On almost a daily basis, developers with large volumes of cash can be found knocking on the doors of Bucks County farmhouses with the intent of buying the rolling hills of farmland and turning the cornfields and pastures into housing developments. Efforts are underway, however, to save the remaining farmlands and preserve the agricultural roots and historic charm of the area.

Wildlife

Despite the rapid residential growth during the past decade, wildlife continues to flourish. Plump, white **geese** and **mallard ducks** flock naturally to the canals and river's edge. **Beaver** activity has been spotted in Point Pleasant, Pennsylvania. **Raccoons, opossums, chipmunks, turkey buzzards, pheasants, foxes, porcupines** and **skunks** make their homes in wooded areas. **Squirrels** are abundant (in Princeton, there are all-black squirrels). And be careful of **deer**; large herds are often seen darting through fields and across residential lawns and highways.

It is not uncommon to see traffic halted in downtown New Hope to allow a duck or goose family to cross the street.

History

The First People

The **Lenni Lenape** ("Original People") were the first to discover the fertile Delaware River valley, settling here in 1397. The Lenape hunted and fished along the Delaware and its tributaries, and today some of the major roads along the river follow their original hunting-and-gathering trails. Early settlers in the area called the Lenape "Delaware Indians" because their many villages flanked both sides of the river.

When William Penn came to the region in the 1600s, he was respectful of the Lenape and, in turn, gained the tribe's loyalty and trust. Following Penn's death, however, tension built as greedy settlers tried to steal the tribe's land. By the 1800s, the Lenape had moved west. Today, only a handful of Lenape Indians remain – all in Oklahoma.

Colonization

 Bucks County was officially founded in 1681 by **William Penn**, who named the colony after Buckingham, the shire in which he was born. The resemblance to England is clear even today. Rolling countryside drops down to the wide Delaware River just as England's does along the Thames; crossroads pubs and stone houses here would look equally at home in the Cotswolds. But the ties to the Motherland stop there.

✖ HISTORIC TRIVIA

The **Liberty Bell** was hidden in Bucks County to prevent the British Army from melting it for ammunition.

In 1776, the region played a pivotal role in turning the tide of the Revolutionary War when **George Washington** led his ragged army across the ice-choked Delaware River to assault the unsuspecting Hessian troops at Trenton. Washington Crossing State Park, just south of New Hope, commemorates the event every December 25th with a re-enactment of the historic event (see page 25).

The 20th Century

In the late 1920s and '30s, the region's bucolic beauty, cheap real estate, proximity to New York City and the lure of country living attracted artistic, literary and theatrical luminaries such as **Oscar Hammerstein II**, **Pearl S. Buck**, **Dorothy Parker** and **James Michener**. The New York media labeled the area "the genius belt." With the artists' arrival came the **Bucks County Playhouse** and a multitude of restaurants, galleries, studios and specialty shops.

★ FAMOUS FACES

The living room of **Dorothy Parker's** house in Pipersville, near Doylestown, Pennsylvania, was painted in 10 shades of red. The writer's carpets were also red, as was her furniture. The idea was so outrageous, so contrary to convention that locals dubbed Parker's "style" **Pipersville Modern**.

Today, the region continues to attract an eclectic group of artists, writers, poets and actors, many of whom make their homes and studios in historic, out-of-the-way fieldstone houses, renovated barns and converted carriage houses.

CELEBRITY WATCH

The following personalities have (or once had) homes in the Delaware River Valley.

- **Peter Benchley**, writer
- **Pierce Brosnan**, actor
- **Pearl S. Buck**, Nobel Prize-winning humanitarian and author
- **Bill Cosby**, actor
- **Albert Einstein**, scientist
- **Harrison Ford**, actor
- **Daniel Garber**, impressionist painter
- **Richard Gere**, actor
- **Oscar Hammerstein II**, writer and lyricist
- **Moss Hart**, playwright
- **Edward Hicks**, primitive painter
- **Peter Jennings**, news anchor
- **George S. Kaufman**, playwright
- **Henry Chapman Mercer**, artist, architect, and collector
- **Toni Morrison**, writer, Nobel laureate
- **Joyce Carol Oates**, writer
- **Dorothy Parker**, poet, humorist, and drama critic
- **S.J. Perelman**, humorist
- **Christopher Reeve**, actor

- ❖ **Nelson Shanks**, realist painter
- ❖ **Ben Solowey**, local artist
- ❖ **Gennady Spirin**, artist and children's book illustrator
- ❖ **Stephen Sondheim**, writer and lyricist

⭐ FAMOUS FACES

Writer **Dorothy Parker** alarmed her neighbors by chopping down ancient trees that were blocking the light outside her home in Pipersville. **Moss Hart**, by contrast, was Bronx-born and dirt-poor until his first Broadway hit, but spent $33,000 planting trees on his Bucks County property.

Getting Here & Getting Around

The Best Time to Visit

 "High season" for travel in the Delaware River Valley area is late spring through fall, with the heaviest concentration of visitors on the weekends. On Sundays in particular, both **New Hope** and **Lambertville** can become a bumper-to-bumper sea of cars, SUVs and pick-up trucks towing boats. If at all possible, try to visit during the week, when many inns offer lower rates and crowds are at a minimum.

★ **TIP**

In New Hope, parking can be especially difficult. Try parking on the side-streets of Lambertville and walking across the iron bridge to New Hope, or park at the New Hope-Solebury High School on Route 179. A sidewalk leads from the school back to town.

By Air

 The Delaware River Valley is easily accessible from two major airports: **Newark International**, ☎ 973-961-6000; and **Philadelphia International**, ☎ 215-937-6800, 215-937-6937, or, for flight information, 800-PHL-GATE. Both airports are served by the major airline carriers.

Lehigh Valley International Airport in Allentown, PA, ☎ 888-FLY-LVIA or 610-266-6000, is also close. Major carriers to Lehigh include **Continental**, ☎ 800-525-0280; **Delta Air Lines**, ☎ 800-221-1212; **Northwest**, ☎ 800-225-2525; **United**, ☎ 800-241-6522; and **US Airways**, ☎ 800-428-4322.

Mercer County Airport in Ewing Township, just 12 miles from Princeton and equally close to Lambertville, offers daily flights from Boston/Hanscom Field via **Shuttle America**, Terminal Circle Drive, ☎ 609-921-3100, www.shuttleamerica.com.

By Car

 New Hope, Pennsylvania and Lambertville, New Jersey are located on the Delaware River between New York City and Philadelphia. Many visitors travel to the area by car, as the region is easily accessible from I-95, I-78, the Pennsylvania Turnpike, and Route 202.

MILEAGE TO/FROM BUCKS COUNTY	
ATLANTIC CITY, NJ	82
BALTIMORE, MD	120
BOSTON, MA	288
HARRISBURG, PA	106
HARTFORD, CT	191
NEW YORK CITY, NY	75
PHILADELPHIA, PA	26
PITTSBURGH, PA	301
ROCHESTER, NY	286
WASHINGTON, DC	158
WILMINGTON, DE	54

State law dictates that an attendant pump your gas in New Jersey.

By Train

Amtrak stops in Philadelphia, Pennsylvania and in Trenton and Princeton, New Jersey; ☎ 800-872-7245.

New Jersey Transit runs a local train from Princeton Junction to New York City ($14 round-trip), and visitors can pick up the "Dinky" train from Princeton Junction to downtown Princeton (or vice versa) for a nominal fee; ☎ 800-772-2222.

By Bus

Trans-Bridge Lines operates daily bus service to Lambertville from the Port Authority in New York City ($24 round-trip), from JFK (about $45 round-trip) and from Newark (about $25 round-trip). Passengers are dropped at Main and Bridge Streets in Lambertville, just one block from the center of town and a short walk across the bridge from New Hope; ☎ 610-868-6001, www.transbridge-bus.com.

New Jersey Transit buses also run between Lambertville and Trenton, where passengers can pick up Amtrak or New Jersey Transit trains; ☎ 800-772-2222.

After Dark

Most restaurants stay open late in summer and on weekends in New Hope and Lambertville, and many of the bars and restaurants feature live entertainment. The farther north you go on both sides of the Delaware, the quieter and more laid back the nightlife.

The restaurant scene is also active in both Doylestown and Princeton – as is theater. Princeton's **Mc-**

Carter Theatre, winner of a Tony Award, is considered one of the best regional theaters in the country. Doylestown hosts a year-round film festival of great black-and-white classic movies.

Alive Guide
Price Scales $

Lodging

During the 1700s, when York Road became the first major highway between New York City and Philadelphia, residents of both Bucks and Hunterdon counties found themselves host to weary travelers. In time, inns and taverns sprang up offering food, lodging and comfort. Many of these inns remain today, offering elegant to rustic river-side accommodations.

The following price scale is intended as a guideline to help you choose lodging best suited to your budget.

ACCOMMODATIONS PRICE SCALE
Price scale is based on a standard room for two persons, per night.
Inexpensive . . . . under $100
Moderate. . . . . $100-$200
Expensive . . . . $201-$300
Deluxe . . . . more than $300

Restaurants

The Delaware River Valley is filled with restaurants, some long-established and informal, as well as boutique and upscale eateries. In each chapter, *Best Places To Eat* includes mini-reviews on select restaurants, while *Culinary Secrets* highlight the shouldn't-miss cheeses, breads, coffees, ice creams, chocolates and other specialties.

DINING PRICE SCALE
Pricing includes one entrée, with glass of wine and coffee.
Inexpensive . . . . under $20
Moderate. . . . . $20-$35
Expensive. . . . . over $35

Shopping

While there is both quirky and upscale shopping, the Delaware River Valley is best known for its **art** and **antiques**. Lambertville, in particular, is known as New Jersey's "Antiques Capital," home to everything from 18th-century furniture and decorative arts to 1950s modern. One-of-a-kind art pieces are also abundant.

Festivals & Events

Festivals – in celebration of shad, ice, antiques and history – are numerous throughout the Delaware River Valley. The following are some of the more notable celebrations.

February

Winter Festival

Winter Festival began in Lambertville as a carnival of outdoor winter activities and has evolved into a two-town weekend extravaganza of visual arts, ice carvings, theater, music and food. Attendees can watch live ice-carving demonstrations by master carvers, then meander through both towns to find completed works. On one journey I spotted an exquisite Eiffel tower outside C'est La Vie, a French bakery in New Hope, and a perfectly carved figure skater in Lambertville, not far from the frozen canal.

Activities include jazz concerts, theatrical events, a parade across the bridge from New Hope to Lambertville (including Philadelphia Mummers and bagpipe bands), a chili cook-off with area chefs, house tours and guided winter walks. Winter Festival is typically held the first weekend of February. ☎ 215-862-2974, www.winterfestival.net.

March

Bucks Fever

The Central Bucks Chamber of Commerce originally launched Bucks Fever as a six-week celebration of visual and performing arts, festivals and history. What seemed an impressive roster of events in 1987 now includes over 250 events running from March through October. To receive a calendar of Bucks Fever events (available in early spring), write to the Central Bucks Chamber of Commerce, 115 W. Court Street, Doylestown, PA 18901, or call ☎ 215-348-3913.

April

Shad Festival

One weekend a year, Lambertville residents sing about shad, draw it, catch it and eat it. The Shad Festival began in 1980 to celebrate the return of the shad to the Delaware River, signaling that the river (after years of pollution) was once again clean. Artists and crafters line the streets in a juried show, chefs show off their culinary talents, and **River-keepers**, a local, non-profit organization, gently reminds festival-goers how to keep the Delaware (as well as other rivers) clean.

Shad Festival is also an opportunity to see the **Lewis Shad Fishery**, where owner Fred Lewis continues the seine-netting tradition his family began in 1888. The fishery is New Jersey's last commercial shad fishery in action. Another highlight of the festival is the **Shad Festival Poster Auction**, which offers original art work donated by local artists from both sides of the Delaware. All monies raised at the auction are used to fund scholarships for high school seniors going on to study art in college. The Shad Festival is held the last weekend in April. Contact the Lambertville Area Chamber of Commerce, 239 North Union Street, ☎ 609-397-0055.

Communiversity

Also known as "Town & Gown," **Communiversity** serves as Princeton's annual spring celebration of the arts. For one day in April, Princeton closes down Nassau Street to traffic – making way for musicians, performing artists, visual artists, craftspeople, storytellers, magicians, singers, dancers, gospel choirs and food vendors. There is an international feel to the event, due largely to the **Princeton University international center**, which has added foods, displays and performances, including a flag procession, to the mix. Communiversity is held during the last weekend of April, and is sponsored jointly by the students of Princeton University and the Arts Council of Princeton. For details, contact the Arts Council

at 102 Witherspoon Street, Princeton, NJ 08542,
☎ 609-924-8777.

May

Mercer Museum Folk Fest

Held the second full weekend in May (Mother's Day
weekend), the Mercer Museum Folk Fest has become a widely heralded event, as museum grounds
are transformed into living history. Skilled, costumed
artisans demonstrate crafts that were a part of ev-
eryday life in early America. All-day entertainment
includes music, jugglers and storytellers. For kids,
there's a hands-on craft tent, mini-farm with animals
and a "granny's trunk" containing old-fashioned
clothing for dressing up. The **6th Pennsylvania
Regiment** returns each year with its Revolutionary
War-era encampment, and special demonstrations
include blacksmithing, broom-making, hearth cooking and shoemaking. 84 South Pine Street (Pine and
Ashland streets), Doylestown, ☎ 215-345-0210. Free
parking at Fonthill Park (Swamp Road and Court
Street) with shuttle bus service.

June

P-rade

The P-rade, held each year during Princeton University's reunion weekend, dates back to 1906 when
reunion planners lined up alumni in an orderly fashion (to prevent the wild rush for the best seats at the

Princeton-Yale baseball game) and marched them to the ball field. Marching bands and exotic floats soon joined. The P-rade was canceled during World War I, resumed in the 1920s, was canceled again during World War II and resumed once more in 1946. In 1968, when Senator Robert Kennedy's funeral train passed through Princeton Junction (just a few miles from campus) on the same afternoon as the P-rade, a debate arose. Some felt the P-rade should be canceled out of respect for the Kennedy family; others thought it should take place as usual. A compromise was made. The baseball game was canceled (and never revived) and the P-rade followed a revised route that kept it on campus. Today, the P-rade continues to amuse with its outlandish black-and-orange costumes and even a menagerie of animals from elephants to tigers. Celebrity P-raders have included such Princeton alumni as former New Jersey Senator Bill Bradley and actors Jimmy Stewart and Brooke Shields. P-rade is held the Saturday before commencement; contact the Princeton University Alumni Association, Princeton, NJ 08544, ☎ 609-258-3000.

July

New Hope Performing Arts Festival

Dedicated to premiering new works, the New Hope Performing Arts Festival was first mounted in 1987 and has rapidly been labeled a cultural gem. Among the festival's successes is the 1992 premiere of *All in the Timing*, a series of one-act plays by David Ives, which moved on to New York and earned Ives a Critics Outer Circle "Playwright of the Year" award.

In 1999, the festival moved to the new, 500-seat **Stephen Buck Memorial Theater** at the New Hope-Solebury High School on Bridge Street. The festival, which runs through July and August with shows on Fridays and Saturdays, previews new works in drama, classical music, children's theater, comedy and choral productions. Advance tickets are recommended. For a schedule, ticket information and reservations, call the New Hope Arts Commission, ☎ 215-862-1699.

August

New Hope Auto Show

Sponsored by the New Hope-Solebury Community Association, this classic auto show is considered to be one of the best in the country. With 40 divisions, the show offers collectors and racing car buffs a chance to reminisce over the cars of their childhoods, view sports cars from all over the world and dream about the Rolls Royces and Bentleys built for royalty. A gala parade of champions ends each day with the prized Governor's cup of the Commonwealth of Pennsylvania presented on Sunday. The show is held at the New Hope-Solebury High School grounds, typically on the second weekend of August. Entry forms and information are available from the New Hope Automobile Show, PO Box 62, New Hope, PA 18938, ☎ 215-862-5665, www.newhopeautoshow.org.

September

Polish-American Festival

This celebration convenes during the first two weekends of September at the **National Shrine of Our Lady of Czestochowa** in Doylestown. The $6 admission fee includes entrance to all festival shows, unlimited rides, polka parties and special exhibits. Polish-American food such as pierogi, placki, kielbasa, golabki, Polish ice, chicken and hoagies are sold, as are religious articles and Polish imports. National Shrine of Our Lady of Czestochowa, 654 Ferry Road, PO Box 2049, Doylestown, PA 18901; ☎ 215-345-0600.

New Hope Film Festival

This film festival made its debut in 2000 with a three-day showing. In its second year, the festival featured 10 films over a seven-day span, and was moved to the New Hope Fire Hall, which seats up to 400. The date of the event varies from late September to early October; contact the New Hope Arts Commission, ☎ 215-862-1699.

October

New Hope Arts & Crafts Festival

Held on the first weekend in October, this juried show features nearly 200 artists and craftsmen from around the country. Streets are blocked off, with artisans exhibiting their wares – photography, pottery, jewelry, wearable art – throughout town. Contact the New Hope Visitors Center, ☎ 215-862-5030 (to speak to staff) or 215-862-5880 (for automated information).

Pumpkin Fest

The main draw of this event, held on the grounds of the Moravian Pottery and Tile Works in Doylestown on the weekend before Halloween, is the pumpkin carving – and nighttime illumination. Artists arrive early on Saturday morning and start carving the huge (Atlantic Giant) pumpkins, which range from 100 to 300 pounds. Carving stops late in the day and the newly transformed pumpkins – with themes of Cinderella, Medusa and Dracula, among others – are lit both Saturday and Sunday nights. Also onsite is a petting zoo, children's rides and games, food and bluegrass music. The event is co-sponsored by the Bucks County Council on Alcoholism and Drug Dependence; Bucks County Department of Parks and Recreation; and the Bucks County Historical Society. Hours are noon to 9 p.m. both days. Admission is $3 children; $5 adults. Contact the Bucks County Council on Alcoholism and Drug Dependence, ☎ 215-345-6644.

November

Day of the Dead Celebration

In honor and recognition of Princeton's fast-growing Hispanic population, the Princeton Arts Council started a community-wide celebration of *El Día de los Muertos* in 2000. Held at the Arts Council building on November 2, the festive party commemorates the Mexican holiday and features altars constructed by local schoolchildren, live Mexican music, performances by Ballet Folklórico dancers, storytelling, food and sugar-skull decorating. Admission is free. Princeton Arts Council, 102 Witherspoon Street, Princeton, NJ 08542, ☎ 609-924-8777.

December

Re-enactment of Washington's Crossing

Every December 25th, thousands of people line both sides of the Delaware to watch a re-enactment of General George Washington's icy Christmas Day 1776 crossing, which scored a decisive victory in the Revolutionary War. The re-enactment began in 1952, and has been held every Christmas Day since, regardless of weather conditions. In fact, the more inclement the weather, the more re-enactors like it.

Washington's troops began their quarter-mile crossing at 6 p.m. on December 25, 1776 but did not finish until 3 a.m. due to the bitter cold weather and floating chunks of ice on the river. The troops – 2,400 soldiers, 200 horses and 18 cannons – then proceeded eight freezing miles downstream to surprise Hessian mercenaries celebrating Christmas in Trenton, New Jersey.

The re-enactors begin their journey at noon at Washington Crossing State Park (just south of New Hope on Route 32), and finish just across the river in Titusville, New Jersey (just south of Lambertville on Route 29), with ceremonies held on both sides. Washington Crossing State Park, ☎ 215-493-4076.

Information Sources

Bucks County Conference & Visitors' Bureau
152 Swamp Road
Doylestown, PA 18901
☎ 215-345-4552
www.buckscountycvb.org

Hunterdon County Chamber of Commerce
2200 Route 31, Suite 15
Lebanon, NJ 08833
☎ 908-735-5955
www.hunterdon-chamber.org

Chamber of Commerce of the Princeton Area
216 Rockingham Row
Princeton, NJ 08540
☎ 609-520-1776
www.princetonchamber.org

New Hope

Beauty should guide all who paint. – Edward Redfield

History

In his book *Michener and Me* (Running Press, Philadelphia and London, September 1999), Bucks County author **Herman Silverman**, who shared a 50-year friendship with the Pulitzer Prize-winning writer, reminisces about some of the old New Hope luminaries:

> "In the summertime during the late '40s, on most Saturdays our house was bustling late into the night with show-business people who were performing at the Bucks County Playhouse, which was going full tilt in nearby New Hope, or at the Music Circus, a summer theater just across the Delaware River in Lambertville, New Jersey. Ann and I would spread the table with cold cuts and snacks and open up the house. The theater crowd was drawn by the food, the fun and our swimming pool, one of the few around at the time. The "big shots" (Hammerstein, Kaufman, Hart) weren't frequent guests at our parties but the "little shots" were. Then-aspiring actors such as George C. Scott, Walter Matthau, and Janis Paige would join us at the gatherings. Jim (Michener) often showed up at these late-night parties. But

few knew much about him, as he had not yet won the Pulitzer Prize."

New Hope, for decades, has been labeled "artsy" – a haven for artisans working in tiny studios and lofts overlooking the river; a respite for Broadway and NYC performers. Many visitors are surprised to learn that the town's roots are actually industrial.

The Beginnings of Industry

By the early 1700s, New Hope – blessed with the geography of the river valley – was already home to a fulling mill (for shrinking cloth), a rolling and splitting mill (which cut strips of metal to make nails), a grist mill, woolen and flaxen mills, and an iron foundry. In 1781, a newcomer named **Benjamin Parry** purchased 16.5 acres of property in Coryell's Ferry (as New Hope was then called), and in the decade that followed increased his land holdings to encompass almost all of what is today New Hope. The young entrepreneur owned and operated mills that produced linseed oil, flaxseed oil, lumber and flour on both sides of the river. When his Coryell's Ferry mill burned to the ground in 1790, Parry rebuilt the grist mill and sawmills and called them "The New Hope Mill." Shortly after, the town's name changed to **New Hope**.

The Canal Opens

In 1832, the opening of the **Delaware Division Canal** gave the manufacturers of New Hope a faster method – mule-drawn barges – to distribute their goods. During the canal's heyday, 3,000 mule-drawn barges traveled the route between Bristol and Easton, Pennsylvania, carrying Bushkill whiskey, iron ore and more than one million tons of coal per year. Ultimately, the railroad diminished the use of waterways as major lines of trade, and New Hope faded into obscurity. But not for long.

The Artists Arrive

 By the end of the 19th century, the natural lull of the river and beauty of the landscape attracted a new breed of entrepreneurs – landscape painters. Many of the artists who came to paint stayed, and before long, New Hope was perceived as an "art colony." The artists, influenced by French Impressionism, soon became known as the **New Hope School** painters (or **Pennsylvania Impressionists**). They found the natural beauty of the river – and canal especially – ideal subjects and painted outdoors even during severe weather.

New Hope

☛ **DID YOU KNOW?**

On windy days, Pennsylvania Impressionist **Edward Redfield** (1869-1965) used to strap his canvases directly to trees. "When I first began to work," Redfield wrote, "most artists used models in studios. What I wanted to do was to go outdoors and capture the look of the scene, whether it was a brook or bridge as it looked on a certain day. I trained myself to set down what I saw in one day and never painted over my canvases again. I think it ruins them. Either you got it the first time or you haven't."

A main source of inspiration in Bucks County has always been the region's picturesque pastures, streams, farmhouses and colonial villages.

Writers and actors soon followed, and by the 1920s and '30s New Hope was home to an impressive list of theatrical and literary personalities, among them Moss Hart, Oscar Hammerstein II, Pearl S. Buck, George Kaufman, Dorothy Parker, Nathanael West, S.J. Perelman, and native son James Michener. From this theatrical enclave came the inspiration for the Bucks County Playhouse.

★ **FAMOUS FACES**

Moss Hart married well-known actress and singer **Kitty Carlisle** in New Hope.

Benjamin Parry's then-250-year-old gristmill had long stood idle and there was talk of demolishing it to make room for riverside development. A group of townspeople formed the **New Hope Association** to save the mill. The Thespians joined forces, and in 1939 they transformed the mill into a summer theater; during the 1940s and '50s the Bucks County Playhouse attracted even more artists to the area.

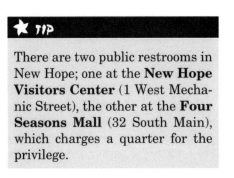

Sunup to Sundown

Although New Hope is less than one square mile and has only four main streets, it offers an array of things to see and do. The following are among the more notable attractions.

> **★ TIP**
>
> There are two public restrooms in New Hope; one at the **New Hope Visitors Center** (1 West Mechanic Street), the other at the **Four Seasons Mall** (32 South Main), which charges a quarter for the privilege.

Walking & Biking

Ghostly Lantern Walks

"Right here... the Phantom Hitchhiker has been spotted." The tour guide raises her colonial-style

New Hope

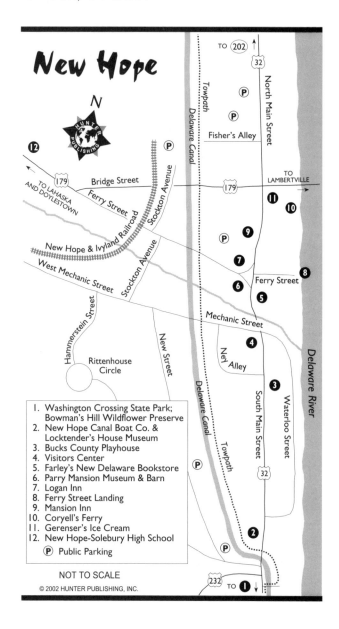

1. Washington Crossing State Park;
   Bowman's Hill Wildflower Preserve
2. New Hope Canal Boat Co. &
   Locktender's House Museum
3. Bucks County Playhouse
4. Visitors Center
5. Farley's New Delaware Bookstore
6. Parry Mansion Museum & Barn
7. Logan Inn
8. Ferry Street Landing
9. Mansion Inn
10. Coryell's Ferry
11. Gerenser's Ice Cream
12. New Hope-Solebury High School

   Ⓟ Public Parking

NOT TO SCALE

© 2002 HUNTER PUBLISHING, INC.

lantern, creating an eerie shadow across her face. "I've seen him myself." A young girl gasps. "He's a young man, with very blond hair and blue eyes. He wears a brown jacket and carries a knapsack. It is said that he was killed late at night."

The hitchhiker is just one of many ghosts believed to walk New Hope's narrow alleyways and haunt its centuries-old houses. **Joseph Pickett** – a late-19th-century artist – has reportedly been spied all over town, as has **Aaron Burr** (Vice President of the United States under Thomas Jefferson). Burr hid out in New Hope after killing **Alexander Hamilton** in a New Jersey duel. There are also tales of baby screams, vacuum cleaners running while unplugged and mysterious bell ringers. Advance reservations are recommended near Halloween.

New Hope's lantern walks are best experienced on a crisp autumn night.

To participate, contact **Ghost Tours**, ☎ 215-957-9988. Walks begin at 8 p.m. at the cannon in the center of town on Saturday nights, June through August; Friday and Saturday nights, September through November. Tours are $8 per person.

☞ DID YOU KNOW?

The ghost of Aaron Burr, former Vice President of the United States, is said to hang out at New Hope's Havana Restaurant.

Art & Architecture Tour

This 90-minute walking tour was introduced in 2000 by art historian **Dr. Lori Verderame**, director of Masterpiece Galleries (see page 44). The tour highlights the history of the New Hope art colony and its artists, as well as the river and canal. There is also focus on New Hope's Colonial, Federal and Victorian architecture. Admission is $10 for adults; ages 16 and under free. The tours are held Saturdays and Sundays, April through October, and meet at Masterpiece Galleries, 15 West Mechanic Street, ☎ 215-862-4444.

Self-guided Tour

More than 45 buildings in New Hope date back to the late 1700s.

Grab an espresso and baguette from **C'est La Vie** (French bakery), then stop by the **New Hope Visitor's Center** or **Gerenser's Ice Cream** for a self-guided tour map ($4) and start walking. Learn about the town's history, colorful "characters," and past and present-day artisans. Call the New Hope Visitor's Center, ☎ 215-862-2050 for private tours.

Along the Canal

The Delaware Canal was dug by hand between 1827 and 1832 and remained in commercial operation until 1932.

One of New Hope's greatest natural assets – the **Delaware Canal** – is free and easily accessible from any point as it runs straight through town. During the 19th century, the canal was used to transport products from the interior sections of Pennsylvania to Philadelphia and New York City. Today, it serves solely as a source of recreation – and inspiration. Even on the busiest days, visitors can find solitude and tranquility walking or biking the towpath, much like the New Hope Impressionists who used to paint here.

★ TIP

The towpath appears to terminate at the south end of New Hope, but it doesn't. Walkers and cyclists wishing to continue southward (toward Washington Crossing State Park) should cross South Main Street (Route 32), follow the gravel road next to the canal all the way through the parking lot of Odette's Restaurant, cross the small bridge just south of Odette's and pick up the towpath again as it passes the Waterworks condominium complex.

New Hope

Historic Sites

Benjamin Parry Mansion

Go behind the white picket fence for a look inside the fieldstone mansion built by **Benjamin Parry** upon his arrival in New Hope in 1784. The mansion remained in the Parry family for almost two centuries until being purchased and restored by the New Hope Historical Society in 1966. Behind the mansion is **Parry Barn**, which has been converted into an art gallery (see page 43). Both house and barn are open May through December, Friday through Sunday, 1-5 p.m. 45 South Main Street, ☎ 215-862-5652.

Locktender's House Museum

Four hand-painted murals at Lock #11 trace the history of the canal from the late 1820s.

Experience canal life as it existed 150 years ago inside this restored 19th-century Locktender's House. A permanent exhibit, *Life at the Lock*, depicts canal workers and their families at work and play. The museum is open weekdays, between 10 a.m. and 4 p.m. 145 South Main Street (at the New Hope Mule Barge Ride), ☎ 215- 862-2021.

Washington Crossing State Park

Two miles south of New Hope is the site where, in 1776, General George Washington led his ragged troops across icy waters for a surprise attack on the Hessians. Today, it is Washington Crossing State Park, and offers a recreational sanctuary on both sides of the river. Pennsylvania-side highlights include **Bowman's Hill Tower**, a 100-foot observatory built in the 1930s to commemorate the lookout of the American Revolution (an elevator is available for less energetic visitors). Another attraction is **Bowman's Hill Wildflower Preserve**, with seemingly endless trails of indigenous wildflowers and plants. 1112 River Road (Routes 32 and 532, three miles north of I-95 Exit 31), Washington Crossing, PA 18977; ☎ 215-493-4076.

In summer, on the New Jersey side, the Park's **Open Air Theater** (see page 114) features outdoor community theater productions.

Scenic Routes

Roads that move and carry us where we wish to go.
  – Blaise Pascal, 17th-century French philosopher

Riverboats, mule-barges, railcars and horses were all part of New Hope's vibrant history, and visitors can still experience these.

Mule-Barges

Commercial mule-barging halted in 1932, and in that same year tourist mule-barge rides started. Spanish-Columbian Leo Ramirez and German George Schweidkhardt have owned **New Hope Mule Barge** since 1976. At their outlying farm, they care for the nine mules that draw their four barges two miles upstream to the Route 202 bridge and back. A musician-historian relates canal lore and strums folk songs. Excursions last one hour, and run daily, May to October. ☎ 215-862-2842.

New Hope Canal Boat Company also offers one-hour mule-barge excursions. Boats depart on Fridays, Saturdays and Sundays in April, and daily from May through October. The cost is $7.95 for adults, $6.50 for children under 12; 149 South Main Street, New Hope, ☎ 215-862-0758.

Riverboat Rides

Captain Robert Gerenser (of Gerenser's ice cream fame) offers rides aboard his 65-foot, Mississippi-style stern paddlewheeler daily, from May through September; the cost is $5 for adults, $3 for children under 12. Coryell's Ferry, 22 South Main Street, ☎ 215-862-2050.

Wells Ferry runs narrated historic tours up and down the Delaware aboard a pontoon boat; the cost is $6 for adults, $4 for children. Ferry Street Landing on the river, ☎ 215-862-5965.

THE GREAT FLOOD OF '55

In August of 1955, the Delaware River broke its banks and flooded New Hope, as a result of back-to-back hurricanes. People reported banging knees on the top of parking meters while "swimming" on Main Street. Inside the Bucks County Playhouse, waters rose two inches above the stage and box-office counter.

Horse-Drawn Carriage Rides

Bucks County Carriages offers 20-minute horse-drawn carriage rides through New Hope. The fee is $12 for adults, $6 for children; sign up in front of The Logan Inn (see page 57). For a special treat, ask about catering services. The rides are a favorite for engagements and weddings. 2586 North River Road, ☎ 215-862-3582.

The New Hope & Ivyland Railroad allows passengers to ride aboard the locomotive while it is pulling the train.

Vintage Rail Excursion

New Hope & Ivyland Railroad offers a 4½-mile, 45-minute round-trip excursion from New Hope to Lahaska aboard a restored 1920s railcar; the ride takes passengers on a slow-moving journey to Peddler's Village and back. The train is pulled by an authentic Baldwin steam locomotive or historic diesel locomotive.

Excursions run daily, May through November, and on weekends during the remainder of the year. The cost is $9.95 for adults; $8.95 for seniors; $5.95 for children ages two and up; $1.50 for children under two. Do check the schedule, though, because special trains are offered throughout the year, including a song and story hour train; a train robbery; fall foliage trains; dinner excursions; and Santa Express trains. New Hope & Ivyland Railroad, 32 West Bridge Street (at Stockton Avenue), ☎ 215-862-2332, www. newhoperailroad.com.

☞ DID YOU KNOW?

The **New Hope & Ivyland** train follows the route filmed in the 1914 silent-movie series, *The Perils of Pauline*, in which the villain tied pretty Pauline to the tracks and her hero saved her at the last second from certain death.

Parks & Gardens

Nature Trails

Bowman's Hill Wildflower Preserve, located 2½ miles south of New Hope on River Road, showcases more than 1,000 species of plants and flowers – all native to Pennsylvania.

There are more than 24 trails, and visitors are free to roam the preserve's 100 acres. The experience changes with the season. Spring brings a profusion of woodland flowers; summer features blooming meadows and cool forests; autumn is great for foliage; and winter trails are highlighted by bright berried shrubs. Guided tours are offered every day at 2 p.m. (except December through February) and cost $3 per person or $5 per couple. Free trail maps and "Seasonal Blooming Guides" are available for those wishing to explore on their own. Bird walks, led by a local naturalist/ornithologist, are held Saturday mornings at 8 a.m. from April through June. A "Wildflower Weekend" is held the last weekend of April and features two days of wildflower walks, workshops and special programs. 1635 River Road, ☎ 215-862-2924.

Recreation

Fly-Fishing

Visitors can experience great fishing on the Delaware River. Catch includes shad in April, striped bass and herring in May, and smallmouth and largemouth bass through October. Guides from **New Hope Fly Fishing** take fishermen and -women out on the river for half- or full-day treks. For novices or those who haven't fished in a while, owner Michael Mullaney runs a fly-fishing school. 48 Ferry Street, New Hope; ☎ 215-862-6896, www.flyfishnewhopepa.com.

Arts & Theater

Long a noted art colony, New Hope continues its affinity for the arts via visual, performing and literary works. These are among the must-sees and -do's.

Performing Arts

The Bucks County Playhouse

The Bucks County Playhouse opened on July 1, 1939 and, in the 60-plus years since, has had nine producers – each adding a different touch to the operation. The grist-mill-turned-theater has served as a resident company, a State Theater of Pennsylvania and tryout center for new plays, a venue for current Broadway shows, and as a summer-only theater.

In the 1970s, the theater, barely afloat, was sold to its current producer **Ralph Miller**, who hired non-equity performers for popular musicals. The mostly-musical lineup continues today with such shows as *South Pacific*, *Grease*, *Carousel*, *Gypsy*, *Annie* and others. 70 South Main Street, New Hope, PA 18938, ☎ 215-862-2041, www.buckscountyplayhouse.com.

★ FAMOUS FACES

Grace Kelly made her theatrical debut at the Bucks County Playhouse in 1949 in *The Torch Bearers*. **Julie Harris** debuted years later (1964) in *The Hostage*.

Concordia Chamber Players

If you're lucky enough to be in town during a Concordia Chamber performance, don't miss it. This high-caliber group was founded by cellist and New Hope native **Michelle Djokic**, who made her professional debut at the age of 13 with the Philadelphia Orchestra and graduated from the Juilliard School of Music at age 20. Djokic made her Carnegie Hall debut in 1985 as a soloist with the New Jersey Symphony. Concordia Chamber concerts are held periodically throughout the year at the New Hope-Solebury High School's **Steven Buck Theater**, ☎ 215-297-5972, www.concordiaplayers.com.

Fine Arts

Art Galleries

New Hope is known for its galleries, which dot Main Street and the surrounding streets. Most galleries are open Tuesday through Sunday, but schedules vary according to summer, holidays and fair weather. Call individual galleries for their hours and exhibit schedules.

NEY ALLEY

Ney Alley (named after New Hope artist Bill Ney) was the original meeting place for painters of the **New Hope School**. It was here that Impressionists would set up their easels and paint outdoor landscapes of the canal – during all four seasons.

The **Ney Museum** houses the works of artist-in-residence **Milt Sigel** in Studio 1, while Ney Alley serves as home to **Masterpiece Galleries**. In the tradition of the New Hope School, contemporary artists have painted a grand mural over the gallery entranceway, reflecting the School's favorite subject matter – the canal. 85 Ney Alley, ☎ 215-862-9032.

When the "open" sign is out, visitors are welcome inside artist-in-residence Milt Sigel's Studio 1.

New Hope

☞ **DID YOU KNOW?**

Impressionist **Bill Ney** is remembered as one of New Hope's finest (his work hangs in the Museum of Modern Art) and most eccentric artists. Ney supplemented his artist's income by working in a local brickyard, and each day would come home from work with part of his pay in bricks. When he had collected enough bricks, he built the Ney Museum to house his artistic works.

PARRY BARN
Behind the Benjamin Parry mansion is Parry Barn, which, like the house, has been restored by the New Hope Historical Society and converted into an art gallery. The Parry Mansion and Barn are open May through December, Friday through Sunday, 1-5 p.m. 45 South Main Street, ☎ 215-862-5652.

HARVEY GALLERIES
"Gabrielle is our smallest (sculpture); we call her Gabby. Diana, of course, is our flagship and she is simply gorgeous." Cameron Harvey, a slightly built, bearded man, points to two sculpted metal foun-

tains. He then moves on to more abstract wall pieces. Only three men (all members of the Harvey family) sculpt, hammer, paint and sell the gallery's incredible showcase of works. And don't expect to find duplicates of anything here. According to Cameron, the Harveys thrive on customers' sketchy ideas, and approximately 70% of their business is custom work. 132 South Main Street, ☎ 215-862-2989.

MASTERPIECE GALLERIES

Dr. Lori Verderame, who introduced New Hope's art and architectural walks, directs this fine art gallery. The art historian also provides art-investment advice and appraisals, and conducts educational lectures. A new museum-quality exhibition opens on the first Friday of every month. 15 West Mechanic Street, ☎ 215-862-4444, www.Masterpiece-Galleries. com.

LACHMAN GALLERY

This unusual gallery features the original works of nationally acclaimed pastel artist Al Lachman, as well as other outstanding artists. Interspersed among the original paintings, serigraphs and prints, are eclectic antiques and oriental rugs. 39 North Main Street, ☎ 215-862-6620, www.lachmanstudios.com.

J&W GALLERY

Winner of the 1998-1999 Arty award for Best Art Gallery in New Hope, J&W features more than 25 local, national and international artists in various mediums. The space is sophisticated, with comfortable seating and dramatic lighting; soft jazz makes viewing a pleasure. 20 West Bridge Street, ☎ 215-862-5119, www.jwgallery.com.

NAGY GALLERY

A relatively new gallery, Nagy features the work of Delaware River Valley artists. Original works include oils, watercolors, sculpture, blown glass, photography and stained glass. New exhibits bimonthly. 16 West Bridge Street, ☎ 215-862-8242.

☛ DID YOU KNOW?

Native son **Joseph Pickett** put New Hope on the artistic map in the early 1900s with his painting, *Manchester Valley*, now in the permanent collection of the Museum of Modern Art in New York City.

Crafts Galleries

TOPEO GALLERY OF FINE AMERICAN CRAFTS

Formerly located in New York City's Greenwich Village, Topeo Gallery of New Hope has been voted one of the top 10 American craft galleries in the US. The gallery, now in two locations on North Main, offers a huge selection of one-of-a-kind art glass, jewelry, fountains, fireplace screens, stained glass and exotic wood. Topeo Gallery, 35 North Main Street, ☎ 215-862-2750; and Topeo South, 15 North Main Street, ☎ 215-862-4949.

MILAGROS GALLERY

The doggie in the window will capture your eye, as will the bright acrylic-colored lizards, armadillos, chickens, rabbits, and cats. Milagros handles only authentic Mexican folk art from Oaxaca. The people of Oaxaca have carved toys and masks for hundreds of years, but it is only recently that their magical wood carvings have captured the imaginations of collectors and enthusiasts all over the world. Unsurpassed for originality and wizardry, Oaxacan wood carvings have become a prized folk art, and Milagros offers one of the best selections in the area. 13 West Mechanic Street, ☎ 215-862-3575.

HEART OF THE HOME
A sign saying "please touch" is the first indication that this is no ordinary gallery. The second is the home-like setting. The works of more than 400 artisans are featured in this 1795 building. Selections include handmade pottery, wrought iron, jewelry, kaleidoscopes, fountains, musical instruments and garden accessories. 28 South Main Street, ☎ 215-862-1880, www.heartofthehome.com.

A MANO GALLERIES
I once bought a hat here – handcrafted of course, as is everything in the store. One of New Hope's oldest craft galleries, A Mano remains a perennial favorite among locals and visitors alike. The shop features accessories for the home and office; kaleidoscopes; jewelry, including custom-made wedding and commitment bands; clothing; glass; clay; garden accessories; and iron furniture. 128 South Main Street, ☎ 215-862-5122, www.amanogalleries.com. Also in Lambertville at 36 North Union Street, ☎ 609-397-0063.

THREE CRANES GALLERY
Two galleries in one, featuring art, oriental antiques, Tibetan statues, wearable art, jewelry and clothing.

More than 20 local and international artists are represented. 82 South Main Street, ☎ 215-862-5626.

ZEPHYR GALLERY
There's a little bit of everything in this crafts gallery, which is rated one of the top 100 in the US. Selections include art jewelry, wearable art, glass, pottery, wood, sculpture, lamps, clocks and furniture. 107 South Main Street, ☎ 215-862-4365.

Shop Till You Drop

New Hope reminds me of Europe. People walk here. It's good to see people walking on the street.

– Joel Vitart, New Hope business owner

If it exists, New Hope sells it – and tourists buy it. Over the years, New Hope has become almost honky-tonk touristy in some of its boutiques and specialty shops. Entire stores are now devoted to windchimes or dog and cat paraphernalia, such as Bow-Wow Dog Lovers Emporium and Meow Cat Lovers Emporium. In this section, we explore some of New Hope's outrageous, upscale, eclectic and specialty shops.

Stores are typically open daily, 11 a.m. to 6 p.m, with longer hours in the summer and on holidays, unless otherwise noted. That said, hours are not written in stone. As one shopkeeper warned me, "There aren't really any set hours in town. If the town's busy, we may stay open as late as 11 p.m. If it's an off-day, we close early."

✗ WARNING!

New Hope is testing "smart meters," which immediately recog-
nize a vehicle's departure from a
parking space and reset themselves to zero. If you're out of
change, the best bet is to park at
the New Hope-Solebury High
School and walk.

Clothing

LOVE SAVES THE DAY

For vintage clothing and collectibles, this is the
place. This two-story shop is chock-full of old prom
gowns, furs, '70s platform shoes, Betty Boop and Su-
perman collectables, kitschy desktop hula dancers –
you name it. 1 South Main Street, ☎ 215-862-1399.
Frequent late hours.

STERLING'S

Featuring elegant attire, handbags and jewelry, this
New Hope staple has grown in popularity over the
years. Although it is often buzzing with brides,
bridesmaids and mothers-of-the-bride in search of
the perfect dress, Sterling's is by no means a bridal
shop. The racks and racks of designer evening
gowns are atypical of the usual department store offerings. 1 North Main Street, ☎ 215-862-3444.

Cosmetics & Beauty

SCARLETT
Proprietor Scarlett Messina takes pride in offering the finest skincare, haircare, cosmetics and fragrance products from around the world – including her own signature collection of makeup in trendsetting colors. Scarlett has hard-to-find Swiss beauty creams, Chinese skincare lines and organic skincare treatments from the UK. 129 South Main Street, ☎ 800-862-2311. The boutique has a location in Philadelphia as well.

LA BELLA VITA
After hours of walking and exploration, there's nothing better than a massage. But this is New Hope, so don't expect just the usual spa.

In Italian, La Bella Vita means "The Beautiful Life," a fitting concept for this tiny, two-story holistic skincare studio, located in one of New Hope's historic houses. Candles, soft music, and tiny twinkling white lights create a warm, welcoming environment.

Check out the bathroom at La Bella Vita, handpainted by a local artist.

"La Bella Vita is more about soul care than beauty care," says owner Candace Griesel. "It's a place where you just leave everything at the door for an hour-and-a-half and rejuvenate."

Candace is well-known for her custom-blended facial masques, using Jurlique and other quality skin-care lines. But her signature treatment is a velvet-stone facial, which combines hot stone massage with crystals and semi-precious stones such as amethyst, turquoise and quartz for chakra balancing. Massage, reflexology and waxing are also provided.

New Hope

23 West Ferry Street, ☎ 215-862-7008. By appointment only.

Specialty Foods

SUZIE HOT SAUCE

Suzie's features hot sauces, hot salsas, even hot pretzels. Check out the *Wall of Flame*, featuring photos of more than 2,000 customers reacting after taste-testing Suzie's merchandise. 19A West Bridge Street, ☎ 800-GO-SAUCE or 215-862-1334, www.suziehotsauce.com.

Books

FARLEY'S NEW DELAWARE BOOKSTORE

Maybe it's the stacks upon stacks of books, or the late-night hours. Or maybe it's just Farley's old-fashioned, independent, void-of-latte-and-chainstore ambience. Whatever, the reason, I love this bookstore – more than any other I've visited.

I discovered Farley's in the mid-1980s while wearing my pajama bottoms (true story). I had just moved to New Hope and, unable to sleep, threw a sweatshirt over my PJs and took a walk. At nearly midnight, on a snowy night, I spotted a light coming from Farley's and entered an eclectic literary paradise that I continue to visit every chance I get. Farley's has a database of more than 70,000 titles (and musical works), with access to more than 400,000 others. Regular hours, Sunday to Thursday, 10 a.m. to 10 p.m.; Friday and Saturday, 10 a.m. to midnight. Summer hours, Sunday to Thursday,

10 a.m. to 11 p.m.; Friday and Saturday, 10 a.m. to midnight. 44 South Main Street, ☎ 215-862-2452, www.farleysbookshop.com.

Gifts

MYSTICKAL TYMES

"This shop has everything a witch needs," one patron told me, and I believe her. Open seven days a week, Mystickal Tymes features altar items, candles, books, tapes, crystals, fountains, herbs, oils and incense, and cauldrons. 127 South Main Street, ☎ 215-862-5629.

PSYCHIC READINGS

New Hope hosts occasional psychic festivals, but tarot and astrological chart readings are available throughout the year. Mystickal Tymes (see above) welcomes walk-ins during the week, and a number of other palm and tarot readers found along New Hope's narrow, twisting side streets take visitors any time.

Just a few doors north, **Gypsy Heaven** – with its blue-and-red neon "Witch Shop" sign in the window – features similar items. 115G South Main Street, ☎ 215-862-5251.

AGAINST THE GRAIN

If medieval items intrigue you, Against the Grain is the place to find armor, swords, knives, alchemy paraphernalia, and medieval clothing and costumes. 82 South Main Street, ☎ 215-862-4800.

GOTHIC CREATIONS

This unusual shop is devoted to more than 400 gargoyles, grave images, architectural elements and angels. All are imported from Europe. 15 North Main Street, ☎ 215-862-2799.

STRAWBERRY JAM

Unique music, jewelry, soaps, aromatics and paper goods. 44C South Main Street, ☎ 215-862-5023.

A LITTLE TASTE OF CUBA

I'd never heard of a certified tobacconist, but this specialty store touting "The Best Cigars in the Free World" reportedly has one. Aside from cigars, you'll find all the necessary accessories: cutters, lighters, and handcrafted humidors. 102 South Main Street, ☎ 215-862-1122.

SPINSTERS RECORDS & TOXIC WASTE DUMP

Thousands of new, used, imported and rare recordings are found here. In the back of the store, there are nearly as many glass bongs. 110 South Main Street, ☎ 215-862-2700.

GROWNUPS

As the name implies, this store is for grownups only, and is definitely a New Hope experience. I went with a friend and came out red-faced and giggling like a schoolgirl. The store has seven rooms of lingerie, cards, adult gifts, videos, leather toys, and other unmentionables. 2 East Mechanic Street, ☎ 215-862-9304.

Housewares

HOT PLATES

Elvis and the 1950s is the theme of this kitschy kitchen store. Items relate to '50s diners and restaurants, and they offer an extensive selection of Fiesta dinnerware. 40 South Main Street, ☎ 215-862-3220.

Throughout New Hope, gas heaters have been installed at outdoor bars and patios, allowing alfresco drinking and dining to begin as early as March. Last call is typically at 2 a.m.

THE HAVANA

This club features live jazz, rhythm and blues, Thursday through Sunday. Ernie, a burly man, tends bar. "Ernie is the rudest bartender in New Hope, but also the best," a regular told me. "This bar is three- , sometimes four-people deep and there's never a wait for a drink." The Havana is also the perfect spot to watch the assortment of tourists walking Main Street. 105 South Main Street, ☎ 215-862-9897.

ODETTE'S

In 1961, Odette Mytril Logan, a Parisian and former stage-and-screen star (best known for her portrayal of Bloody Mary in Broadway's *South Pacific*) renamed this historic tavern "Chez Odette" and turned it into a Country French restaurant.

New Hope

The current owners (the Barbone Family) have preserved the spirit and ambience of the restaurant, now called Odette's, with a piano bar, as well as a cabaret show featuring local, Philadelphia and New York City talent. The cabaret is the longest running on the East Coast. Have dinner beforehand. Reservations necessary. South River Road, ☎ 215-862-2432.

★ FAMOUS FACES

Newscaster **Jessica Savitch** died on October 23, 1983 in New Hope after leaving Chez Odette in a downpour of rain. Her friend mistakenly drove down the towpath leading to the Delaware Canal and the couple drowned, along with Ms. Savitch's Siberian Husky, Chewy.

JOHN & PETER'S

A New Hope classic. More than one rag-torn, hard-rock musician has played in this smoky, no-frills, chips-and-beer setting. Lately though, owners have forgone the grunge in favor of jazz and singer-songwriters. 96 South Main Street, ☎ 215-862-5981.

DOWNSTAIRS AT MOONLIGHT

Around 9 p.m. this casually elegant bistro, located on the lower level of the Moonlight restaurant (see page 60), transforms into a popular nightclub, featuring nightly entertainment. 36 West Mechanic Street, ☎ 215-862-3100.

GAY AND LESBIAN HANGOUTS

There is a definite gay scene in New Hope, and **The Cartwheel** (427 York Road, ☎ 215-862-5575) serves as its hub. Includes a restaurant, bar and club. Also gay-friendly is **The Raven Bar and Restaurant**, 385 West Bridge Street, ☎ 215-862-2081.

UNIQUELY NEW HOPE

Wicca, the religion observed by witches, is practiced in New Hope. On October 30 (the Wiccan New Year's Eve), don't be surprised to see ceremonies being held in open spaces under the moon.

New Hope

Best Places to Stay 🛏

ACCOMMODATIONS PRICE SCALE
Price scale is based on a standard room for two persons, per night.
Inexpensive.....................under $100
Moderate.......................$100-$200
Expensive......................$201-$300
Deluxe ....more than $300

THE MANSION INN
9 South Main Street
New Hope
☎ 215-862-1231
www.themansioninn.com
Expensive to Deluxe

For most of its life, The Mansion Inn, built in 1865, served as a private residence. For 65 years, the whimsical gingerbread mansion was the home of Dr. Kenneth Lieby, affectionately known as the "horse-and-buggy doctor," who delivered more than 3,000 area babies.

When Dr. Lieby retired and moved away, the house fell into disrepair and was earmarked by investors to be gutted and made into a shopping mall. In 1994, Dr. Lieby finally agreed to sell the property – not to investors, but to two preservationists. While the preservationists were not the highest bidders for the property, Dr. Lieby was convinced they'd meet his "other terms" – that being "to preserve the integrity of the house and (Dr. Lieby's) favorite tree." The new owners made good on their promise.

Today, with three guest rooms and five suites, The Mansion Inn features arched doorways, gilded mirrors, fine art and antiques and, yes, Dr. Lieby's favorite tree. Amenities include private baths, turn-down service (with home-baked cookies), afternoon wine and cheese, free parking, feather beds, early-morning coffee and a full gourmet breakfast (choice of french toast du jour or egg dish du jour), plus homemade granola, muffins and fresh fruit. There's a two-night minimum stay on weekends; three nights on holiday weekends.

※ HISTORIC TRIVIA

During restoration of **The Mansion Inn**, workers found comments on the wall of the drawing room, written by workmen in 1865. One read: "John – wallpaperer – '65 – Just heard Lincoln shot – Ford's Theater. Will be all right – hooray for Abe!"

THE LOGAN INN
10 West Ferry Street
New Hope
☎ 215-862-2300
www.loganinn.com
Moderate to Expensive

The historic Logan Inn, reportedly "the most haunted inn in America," underwent a massive restoration and reopened to the public in April 2001. In years past, a glowing, lavender-scented form was said to haunt room #6; a headless Revolutionary soldier occupied the bar, basement and dining room; a little girl appeared in the parking lot; and a man in knee breeches had been seen on the steps to the basement men's room. No word yet if the ghosts like their new digs, which feature private baths and period antiques and furnishings.

The inn was built in 1722, and was then called Ferry Tavern; it is the oldest continuously run inn in Bucks County and one of the five oldest in the United States. The original tavern is still in use. Be sure to check out the wall murals while having a drink. During a 1987 renovation, local artist Tina Dadian uncovered and painstakingly restored them. A more recent 2001 renovation uncovered two cisterns, originally used to collect rainwater. Both of the cisterns (one inside, the other on the front patio) have been preserved and integrated into the new design.

WEDGEWOOD HISTORIC INNS
Aaron Burr House, Umplebe House and
Wedgewood Inn
111 West Bridge Street
New Hope
☎ 215-862-2570
www.new-hope-inn.com
Moderate to Expensive

Families and well-behaved pets will enjoy the child-friendly yet elegant atmosphere of Carl and Dinie Glassman's inns. With their young daughter, Jessica, the Glassmans run a "collection" of three 19th-century houses and live in the back of their 2.5-acre property. Family accommodations include a two-room suite with fireplace, which has a king-size mahogany post bed in the first room and a white iron daybed in the adjoining one; a loft suite with a second bedroom ideal for a child; and a third-floor suite featuring two rooms, Victorian marble bath, wood floors and hand-painted walls. Private couples' quarters and singles are also available. Outdoor porches, hammocks, lawns, and gazebos add to the comfortable ambience.

New Hope

✕ HISTORIC TRIVIA

A 26-foot-long, nine-foot high tunnel found under the Wedgewood Inn is believed to have been part of the **Underground Railroad**. Owner Carl Glassman thinks part of the tunnel was built in the 18th century to store Continental Army ammunition during the American Revolutionary War, and then was extended for use by runaway slaves in the 19th century.

PORCHES
20 Fisher's Alley
New Hope
☎ 215-862-3277
www.porchesnewhope.com
Moderate

Porches, a tiny five-room inn, changed hands in 2001 and has undergone extensive renovation. New owner John Byers, a native of the area and longtime designer and landscaper, is well known for his building renovations. In 1970, Byers built the original Karla's restaurant in New Hope (then named The Apple).

One of Byers' first additions is a second-story wraparound porch accessible from guestrooms via French doors. Inside, carpets have been removed to expose wide-plank, hardwood, pumpkin-pine floors, and elegant antiques appear throughout. The inn is nestled on a quiet alley off North Main Street, and all of the rooms offer canal views.

"We're restoring (Porches) back to the 1800s Federal house that it was," says Byers. The 1830 white-washed brick house was originally built as a granary. During the 1930s, it served as "Pops," a sandwich shop.

Byers is also developing gardens, and plans to convert some of the barns on the property into additional rooms – one catering to those traveling with pets. A full American breakfast is served. Parking is provided but there are no televisions or telephones.

Best Places to Eat

DINING PRICE SCALE
Pricing includes one entrée, *with glass of wine and coffee.*
Inexpensive . . . . under $20
Moderate. . . . . $20-$35
Expensive. . . . . over $35

American

MOONLIGHT
36 West Mechanic Street
☎ 215-862-3100
www.moonlightatnewhope.com
Expensive

New Hope's newest restaurant, Moonlight, may also boast the town's most unusual décor. White is the theme here – goop white to be exact. Designer Jim

Hamilton (also of Hamilton's Grill and The Fish House in Lambertville) describes the creation, "The restaurant is but a canvas. The food and customers are the color." A thousand gallons of "white goop" (joint compound, primer and textured latex paint) were used to seal the restaurant's interior. Books, shelves, chandeliers, and even a piano are sealed under an eerie white cast, as if unearthed from a dig at Pompeii. Juxtaposed throughout the restaurant are 21 three-dimensional "still-lifes" (also "gooped") inspired by the great art masters. Van Gogh-like sunflowers appear in one room; Cézanne-style fruit in another. The chef is Matthew Levine, one of the region's rising stars, who came to Moonlight from Le Bec Fin and Striped Bass in Philadelphia and the famed Ryland Inn in New Jersey. Moonlight's up-scale menu focuses on seafood; a bistro-style menu is served on the lower level in the contrastingly color-ful Downstairs at Moonlight (see page 54).

New Hope

MARTINE'S
7 East Ferry Street
☎ 215-862-2966
Moderate to Expensive

The food is good but the ambience is the prime rea-son for visiting. The tiny stone building that houses Martine's was built in the 1700s – before the Ameri-can Revolution – and operated as a salt store where townspeople purchased salt to preserve their meat. The first-floor bar continues to draw townspeople – locals definitely outnumber tourists. But up the nar-row, rickety, staircase (befitting a 1700s building), the crowd is more mixed. Paintings by local artists line the walls, hanging lamps glow over each small table and exposed wooden beams cradle a peaked ceiling. Try the magret (breast) of duck with pear and Zinfandel sauce, or seafood puff pastry – both regulars on the menu.

> ### ★ CULINARY SECRET
>
> **Country Fair Chocolates** has been dipping chocolate-covered strawberries since it opened nearly 25 years ago. 93 South Main Street, ☎ 215-862-5359.

WILDFLOWER GARDEN & THAI CORNER
8 Mechanic Street
☎ 215-862-2241
Moderate

Wildflower Garden features color-splashed murals of wildflowers painted by New Hope artist Illy Selesnick.

Like real wildflowers, the menu at Wildflower Garden & Thai Corner is eclectic, a rather odd bouquet of Thai, Mexican and old-fashioned home-style cooking.

This restaurant's story began in 1984 when owners Bob Madrick and Grant Waldman left their positions at New York City ad agencies to open a small dessert shop in New Hope. Bob's chunky chocolate cookies (still on the menu) paid the mortgage until approval was granted to open a garden café. Sandwiches and soups were added to the dessert menu, and, soon after that, pot roast, baked chicken, meat loaf and mashed potatoes (recipes from the owners' mothers) made their appearance. In 1997, Grant (a frequent visitor to Thailand), decided to bring classic Thai food to New Hope, and enlisted a Bangkok-born chef who doesn't disappoint. Try the authentic Thai spring rolls, or Gang-Dang red curry in coconut milk and sweet basil, then wash it all down with Singha (imported Thai beer) or a Thai iced tea. As

A branch of Wildflower Garden operates in Chang Mai, Thailand, in the Souvenir Guesthouse.

for the Mexican? Try the Mexican-style corn-on-the-cob topped with mayonnaise, Parmesan cheese and hot sauce.

★ *CULINARY SECRET*

Gerenser's homemade ice cream comes in weird flavors. Choose from African violet, American pumpkin pie, Ukrainian rose petal (it smells like roses), Irish coffee, Puerto Rican banana brandy, Swedish olallieberry, and spicy Caribbean tree bark. 22 South Main Street, ☎ 215-862-2050.

French

LA BONNE AUBERGE
1 Rittenhouse Circle
Village 2 Apartment Complex
☎ 215-862-2462
Expensive

Established in 1972, La Bonne Auberge offers classic French cooking, with Monsieur Gerard Caronello's menu reflecting his culinary training in Lyon, Aix-en-Provence and Paris.

Starters include escargots with garlic and parsley, and lobster tail with brioche and armoricaine sauce. The house salad is memorable for its Dijon-garlic dressing. Meat and fish dishes include darned (filet) of salmon with lobster sauce, and roasted rack of lamb coated with Provençal herbs. The crème brûlée for dessert is as good as it gets.

Presentation is as important as taste here. Tuxedo-shirted servers continually fill water glasses, replace all cutlery with each course, and ensure that entrées arrive at the table under silver domes that are removed in unison.

La Bonne Auberge sits high on a hill; it is set within an apartment complex, but once you leave your car you'd never know it. The gardens are beautiful; the dining room pretty; and the feel is that of a country manor home. Jackets are required. La Bonne Auberge is just outside the center of New Hope off Mechanic Street; call for directions.

★ CULINARY SECRET

Rare gourmet cheeses are the norm at the **New Hope Cheese Shop**. 20 North Main Street, ☎ 215-862-5606.

Italian

LA TERRAZA
18-20 West Mechanic Street (on the Towpath)
☎ 215-862-6121
Moderate to Expensive

During the Revolutionary War, La Terraza restaurant was called The Bloody Bucket, and housed a brothel upstairs.

"I lost a girlfriend over the Spaghetti Alle Vongole," our dark-haired waiter reported as we contemplated the menu. "It's made with clams and lots of garlic, which I love, and she gave me an ultimatum to stop eating it or else. Well, she's gone and I'm still eating the spaghetti."

A thousand white lights, wrapped in grapevines, lead down narrow stairs to this rustic restaurant overlooking the canal. Chef and owner Armando Agnoli has operated restaurants in Fiuggi, Italy (just outside Rome) for decades, and many of his dishes at La Terraza reflect that region's cooking. The wine list features only Italian wines – try the Montepulciano (lighter than a Cabernet). Anything with seafood or veal is excellent, as are the home-made pasta selections. Ask for the tagliatelle (thin, flat noodle) dish with artichokes, as it's not always on the menu. Desserts are also homemade; tiramisu contains Kahlua, while the cheesecake is made with fresh ricotta.

With its rustic Italian ambience and outdoor wrought-iron gazebo, La Terraza is a charmingly romantic wedding spot for up to 125 guests.

New Hope

★ CULINARY SECRET

For great breads, baguettes, and chocolate croissants, go to **C'est La Vie**, run by a former Parisian. 20 South Main Street, ☎ 215-862-1956. Closed Mondays.

Seafood

THE LANDING
22 North Main Street
☎ 215-862-5711
Expensive

Photographs of Switzerland and Norway line the dining room walls of this tiny riverfront restaurant, adding to its European feel. In winter, a glowing fireplace adds to the cozy ambience. But the best view is outside. From late spring to early fall, tables are set up on the outdoor terrace overlooking a scenic stretch of the Delaware River and owners Chris and Ellen Bollenbacher's award-winning gardens.

The Bollenbachers opened The Landing in 1976, and the restaurant has become a New Hope landmark. The wine list is extensive; seafood is the specialty on the seasonal menu. Start with white gazpacho soup, followed by Chilean sea bass or signature porcini-crusted sea scallops (with gingered carrot purée, roasted Italian eggplant, baby spinach and saffron-squash coulis), which appears on the menu from time to time. End your meal with fresh berries and crème caramel.

★ FAMOUS FACES

Dogs on the roof of The Landing have become permanent residents. Look for Chopper, a 12-year-old Chow Chow, on the roof overlooking the 120-seat terrace, and his newest friend, Fred, a two-year-old Bernese mountain dog.

New Hope A to Z

Animal Hospitals

New Hope Veterinary Clinic, 21 North Sugan Road, ☎ 215-862-2909.

Banks

Union National Bank & Trust, 6542 Logan Square, #D, ☎ 215-862-3750.

First Union National Bank, 336 West Bridge Street, ☎ 215-862-9455.

First Federal Savings & Loan, 275 West Bridge Street, ☎ 215-862-5021.

PNC Bank, 2 North Main Street, ☎ 215-862-1524.

Food Markets

Clemens, 322 West Bridge Street, ☎ 215-862-5242.

Giant Food Store, Logan Square Plaza, ☎ 215-862-9060.

WaWa Food Market, 341 West Bridge Street, ☎ 215-862-9330.

Gas Stations

New Hope Mobil, 350 West Bridge Street, ☎ 215-862-5350.

Hospitals

St. Mary Medical Center, Langhorne Newtown Road, Langhorne, ☎ 215-750-2000.

Hunterdon Medical Center, 2100 Westcott Drive, Flemington, NJ, ☎ 908-788-6100.

Movie Theaters

Cinema Plaza, 240 US Highway 202 & 31, Flemington, NJ, ☎ 908-782-2777.

Newspapers

New Hope Gazette, 170 Old York Road, ☎ 215-862-9435.

Bucks County Courier Times, 8400 Route 13, Levittown, PA 19057, ☎ 215-949-4000.

Pharmacies

CVS Pharmacy, New Hope Shopping Center, 302 West Bridge Street, ☎ 215-862-5917.

Eckerd, 6542 Logan Square #H, ☎ 215-862-9228.

Giant Food Store Pharmacy Department, 6542 Logan Square, ☎ 215-862-9065.

Post Offices

New Hope, 325 Bridge Street, ☎ 215-862-2445.

Solebury, 2997 Sugan Road, ☎ 215-297-5503.

Religious Services

Kehilat HaNahar (Reconstructionist Synagogue), 85 West Mechanic Street, ☎ 215-862-1912.

New Hope Religious Science Church, 15 South Main Street, ☎ 215-497-9007.

Old Path Zendo at Rolling Green Farm (Buddhist), 2725 Aquetong Road, ☎ 215-862-5572.

St. Martin of Tours (Roman Catholic), 111 New Street, ☎ 215-862-5472.

St. Phillip's Church, 10 Chapel Road, ☎ 215-862-5782.

Thompson Memorial Presbyterian, 1680 Aquatong Road, ☎ 215-862-2440.

Wine & Spirits

New Hope Winery, 6123 York Road, ☎ 215-794-2331, www.newhopewinery.com.

North of New Hope

Solebury, Centre Bridge, Lumberville, Point Pleasant, and Erwinna

I was thrilled by the beauty of the whole scene. I decided it was the only place to live and work.

– Daniel Garber, Master Artist

Overview

No trip to the Delaware River Valley is complete without a leisurely drive north from New Hope along **River Road** (Route 32), which hugs the Delaware River on the Pennsylvania side and takes you into Solebury and through Centre Bridge, Lumberville, Point Pleasant and Erwinna.

If you didn't know better, you'd swear you were in Europe – the Cotswolds of England, or perhaps the French countryside. Federal-era stone houses dot the twisty road as it passes through tiny, old-fashioned villages, where general stores have miraculously not been replaced by strip malls or fast-food chains.

River Road has been designated by the National Highway Board as one of America's most scenic roads.

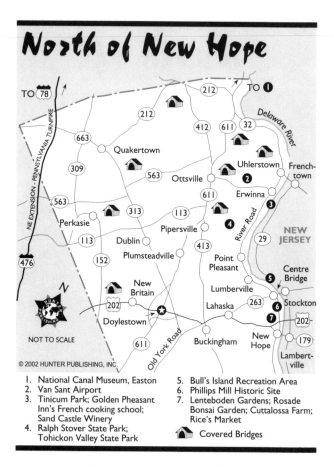

North of New Hope

1. National Canal Museum, Easton
2. Van Sant Airport
3. Tinicum Park; Golden Pheasant Inn's French cooking school; Sand Castle Winery
4. Ralph Stover State Park; Tohickon Valley State Park
5. Bull's Island Recreation Area
6. Phillips Mill Historic Site
7. Lenteboden Gardens; Rosade Bonsai Garden; Cuttalossa Farm; Rice's Market

🏠 Covered Bridges

© 2002 HUNTER PUBLISHING, INC.

NOT TO SCALE

Phillips Mill

The village of New Hope is surrounded by Solebury Township. Whereas New Hope is just one square mile, Solebury Township is 28 square miles.

The first stop on Route 32 just outside New Hope is Solebury, and an even tinier village, Phillips Mill, named for the grist mill built in 1756 by Aaron Phillips. The mill was operated by four generations of the Phillips family until 1894, when the mill, miller's house and adjoining farm were sold to a Philadelphia surgeon. In time, the physician sold the miller's house (across from the mill) to his good friend and painter, **William Lathrop** – inadvertently planting the first seed for the New Hope art colony.

Artist **Edward Redfield** arrived in 1898, settling a few miles north in Centre Bridge; shortly after that, in 1907, artist **Daniel Garber** came to live along Cuttalossa Creek. The three landscape painters formed the first generation of the **Pennsylvania Impressionists**.

In 1908, architect and designer Morgan Colt rebuilt the studio next to Lathrop's house, and completed the "Old English-style" buildings, which today house the Inn at Phillips Mill. You'll know you're there when you reach the hairpin curve.

North of New Hope

☞ DID YOU KNOW?

During the late 1920s, a group of local artists formed the **Phillips Mill Community Association** (☎ 215-862-0582) and purchased the mill for $5,000 to provide the art community a place to exhibit its works. Two exhibits were held per year, along with dances, plays, lectures, dinners and concerts. The Phillips Mill Exhibition is still held today.

Centre Bridge

Just a few miles north of Phillips Mill is Centre Bridge, an equally tiny community, which took its original name of Reading's Ferry from Colonel John Reading, who operated the town's first ferry from 1704 to 1711. A century later, in 1811, the ferry ceased operation and the town was renamed Centre Bridge. A covered bridge opened in 1814, connecting Centre Bridge to Stockton, New Jersey and bringing growth and industry to the area, as well as physicians, blacksmiths, carpenters, an undertaker, shoemakers, and wheelwrights.

☛ DID YOU KNOW?

Centre Bridge's wooden bridge was struck twice by disaster. In 1841, three spans of the bridge were washed away by the river and had to be rebuilt. Although it was the only bridge in the entire area to survive the great flood of 1903, the bridge was struck by lightning in 1923 and was completely destroyed. Impressionist Edward Redfield captured the blaze on canvas. Today, a sturdy steel bridge connects Centre Bridge to Stockton, New Jersey.

Lumberville

 Lumberville is the next town along winding, twisty River Road and, for me, is one of the most picturesque villages in the entire Delaware River Valley. Locked in by the canal, the river and a ridge of mountains, the town is comprised of two rows of beautifully maintained stone and frame houses, a church, a general store/post office, a restaurant/inn and a lumber yard.

Lumberville's first inhabitants (in the early 1700s) were most likely Swedish immigrants, but **Colonel Joseph Wall**, who built two sawmills, is credited with founding the community in 1785. Ten years after the Colonel's death in 1814, the town was appropriately renamed Lumberville, as lumbering and quarrying were the main industries (both still survive today to some degree).

★ TIP

Fill up with gas in New Hope, as there are few gas stations on River Road.

Point Pleasant

Meandering farther north, you'll arrive in Point Pleasant, known today as a recreational haven. River adventures such as tubing and kayaking begin here (see page 78). This village, too, began with a grist mill – grinding grain for soldiers' bread during the Revolutionary War, as well as their gunpowder. In

During the Revolutionary War, residents of the region from Centre Bridge to Point Pleasant were Tory – and loyal to the Crown.

North of New Hope

the early 1800s, a man named **Jacob Stover** came to Point Pleasant, purchasing the grist mill for only 10 shillings at a sheriff's sale. Stover expanded the business and at one point operated more than 28 mills. The property remained in the Stover family for 150 years.

☞ **DID YOU KNOW?**

The last of the Stovers to live on the Point Pleasant mill property were the granddaughters of Ralph Stover, Florence and Clara Louise. The unmarried sisters lived in the house until their deaths in the 1950s, after which time the property was sold. The "Stover girls," as they were called by townspeople, are well remembered for their gift of land for the creation of the **Ralph Stover State Park**, and for the pipe organ that Florence (a music teacher) gave to the local church.

Tinicum & Erwinna

The final leg of River Road (at least for this tour) is from Tinicum through Erwinna. Along this stretch you'll find amazing inns and restaurants (see *Best Places to Stay*, pages 88-92, and *Best Places to Eat*, pages 93-101) and a carefully preserved country-side. Most of these inns were built out of necessity in the 1700s for the rafters and workers building the canal. These men were by all accounts, a rough lot, so it's odd that the inns that served as backdrop for their ale-drinking and brawls are today considered to be among the most civilized and elegant dining and lodging establishments in the area.

Sunup to Sundown

There's more to do than you may first imagine along scenic River Road. After the obvious activities on and around the river and canal towpath, you'll find lots of unexpected things – such as a French cooking school and a winery.

Along the Canal & River

Delaware Canal State Park

One of the prettiest stretches of the towpath lies between New Hope and Erwinna. The park has been named a National Historic Landmark, and the good news for bikers is that a smooth new surface replaces the once-treacherous roots, potholes and rocks that made for a bumpy ride. In many places along this route, the towpath goes right between the river and the canal, making for an especially scenic ride. The towpath serves as a multi-use trail, so expect to encounter walkers, runners, cyclists, dogs, horses and some resident geese. Delaware Canal State Park, 11 Lodi Hill Road, RR 1 Box 615A, Upper Black Eddy, PA 18972, ☎ 888-PA-PARKS or 610-982-5560, www. dcnr.state.pa.us.

North of New Hope

The Lumberville Store (see page 86) rents bicycles and even serves up a picnic lunch to go.

★ TIP

The **Virginia Forest Recreation Area**, on Route 32 north of Centre Bridge, has parking, bathrooms and a picnic area along the towpath.

Pedestrian Bridge

A pedestrian bridge connects Lumberville, Pennsylvania to Bull's Island Recreation Area, on the New Jersey side of the river. This is the area's only footbridge across the Delaware and is accessible from the Black Bass Hotel (see page 90). The bridge offers a rare and peaceful view of the river and an especially romantic setting for after-dinner moonlit walks.

Tubing, Kayaking, & Canoeing

More than 100,000 people per year (from toddlers to senior citizens) negotiate the Delaware River with inner tubes or canoes from Bucks County River Country.

For a day on the river, **Bucks County River Country** rents tubes, kayaks, canoes and rafts. All tours are self-guided, but the company takes you to the drop-off points and picks you up again at the end.

Tubing trips last two, three or four hours, with a stop-off to visit the famous island hotdog man. Rafting trips are six miles long, and average about four hours (but you can take all day). A six-mile canoeing trip averages two hours, while an all-day 12-mile trip stops at towns along the way. Kayaking clinics, single-day and overnight trips are available. Bucks County River Country, 2 Walters Lane, Point Pleasant, ☎ 215-297-5000, www.rivercountry.net.

※ HISTORIC TRIVIA

In the 1980s, historians from the **National Canal Museum** in Easton, Pennsylvania and the **Friends of the Delaware Canal** in New Hope began collecting oral histories of the few surviving canal boatmen – men then in their 70s and 80s who worked the canal as children in the early part of the 20th century. Visitors may listen to these recordings at the Locktender's House Museum in New Hope (see page 36).

Parks & Gardens

Lenteboden Gardens

Located just outside New Hope in Solebury Township, this colorful garden is the business and residence of bulb specialist Charles Mueller. Lenteboden offers an amazing display of daffodils, tulips and hyacinths – all from Holland. The best time to visit, as you may guess, is spring. Charles H. Mueller & Co., 7091 River Road, New Hope, ☎ 215-862-2033.

Rosade Bonsai Gardens

Another must-see garden in Solebury is Rosade Bonsai, one of America's most outstanding bonsai gardens. Classes, lectures and demonstrations are offered (call for schedule), and bonsai supplies, books and tools are sold. Open Friday, Saturday and Sunday, 11 a.m. to 5 p.m. or by appointment. 6912 Ely Road, New Hope, ☎ 215-862-5925.

Cuttalossa Farm

Artist Daniel Garber moved to this picturesque farm on Cuttalossa Road in Lumberville in 1907. He renovated the barn into a studio, dammed the creek to make a pond and lived and worked here for more than 50 years. "To know me, you would have to know this place," he often said. Known as the "Dean of the Pennsylvania Painters," Garber ultimately became one of the most prominent figures in the distinguished group of visual artists living and working in Bucks County. He taught at the Pennsylvania Academy of Fine Arts in Philadelphia for more than 40 years.

Although it is still a private residence, Garber's homestead remains a spiritual, pastoral setting, with the pond and out-buildings welcoming families who bring children to feed the baby Dall sheep and other animals. From River Road, turn onto Cuttalossa Road at the Cuttalossa Inn; the farm will be on your right.

✕ HISTORIC TRIVIA

Painter **Daniel Garber** died in 1958 at his home, Cuttalossa Farm, after falling from his studio balcony while trimming ivy with his son.

Ralph Stover State Park

Ralph Stover State Park, a gift from the "Stover girls" in 1931, encompasses 37 acres of Tohickon Creek valley. The park offers camping, fishing, swimming and miles of wild unspoiled territory to explore. The High Rocks section of the park provides a great view of a horseshoe bend in Tohickon Creek and the surrounding forest. 6011 State Park Road (two miles north of Point Pleasant on State Park and Stump roads), Pipersville, PA 18947; ☎ 800-63-PARKS or 610-982-5560, www.dcnr.state.pa.us.

The cliffs at Ralph Stover State Park are sheer and dangerous, and used only by experienced rock climbers. For your own protection, stay behind the safety rail.

☞ DID YOU KNOW?

The High Rocks portion of **Ralph Stover State Park** was added through the donation of the late James A. Michener.

Tinicum Park

This 126-acre park offers facilities for camping, boating, ice skating and fishing, as well as ball fields and lots of acres to hike. It is the site of many special events throughout the year, including an outdoor antiques show, art festival, dog show and flower show. The park is located on River Road (Route 32) in Erwinna, a few miles south of the Frenchtown Bridge, in Tinicum Township; ☎ 215-757-0571 or 215-348-6114.

North of New Hope

Tohickon Valley Park

Located next to Ralph Stover State Park, Tohickon Valley Park offers 583 acres of hiking trails, trout fishing streams, playgrounds, ball fields and picnic areas. A large swimming pool is available in season. Cafferty Road, Point Pleasant, PA; ☎ 215-757-0571.

Recreation

Scenic Flights

 Just a few turns past EverMay on-the-Delaware (see page 92) is the **Van Sant Airport**. This small country airport offers biplane, glider and aerobatic rides aboard vintage aircraft, as well as hot-air balloon rides. The airport was chosen as one of America's best turf strips by *Private Pilot* magazine. Reservations are necessary. 516 Cafferty Road (off Headquarters Road), Erwinna, PA; ☎ 610-847-8320.

Antique Carousel

Lahaska's Philadelphia Toboggan Company carousel is one of the grandest ever produced. Only 26 such carousels still exist.

Although this museum-quality carousel is about five miles from Centre Bridge (take Greenhill Road to Peddler's Village in Lahaska), it is worth putting on your agenda. In January 1998, Earl Jamison, owner of Peddler's Village (see page 86), found a 1922 Philadelphia Toboggan Company carousel in deplorable condition. Master carver Ed Roth, from Long Beach, California, was commissioned to custom-carve 46 figures in basswood using the traditional techniques of master carvers from a century ago. In July 1998, the fully restored carousel was installed at Peddler's Village. During the restoration, Roth was instructed to reproduce some of the greatest carousel figures ever carved. The outside-row jumpers have delicate manes, real horsehair tails, and as many as 50 glass jewels inlaid in their beautiful trappings. There are menagerie animals as well, including a lion, goat, giraffe, spotted hog and two rabbits. The carousel is fully operational, and rides are $1.50 per person. Peddler's Village, Routes 202 and 263, Lahaska, PA; ☎ 215-794-8960.

During half-time at Tinicum Park's polo matches, spectators can help repair the field by stomping the divots back into place.

Polo Matches

Further proof of the area's British ties are the Saturday polo matches held from May to October at **Tinicum Park** (see page 81). During the match, an announcer explains the rules of the game and describes different aspects of polo. Tailgating is permitted (cars $5); and sitting space is available under a tent on the north side of the announcer's booth, on a first-come basis. Children (and adults) who would like to see what it's like to swing a mallet at a polo ball can do so at half-time while sitting on Charlie Chukker – the Tinicum Park Polo Club's steel horse. Tinicum Park, Erwinna. Polo Hot Line, ☎ 908-996-3321.

North of New Hope

Food & Wine

French Cooking School

Wearing a full-white apron, bare legs peeking out from behind, French-born Michel Faure greets his class of 10 or so at the **Golden Pheasant Inn**, where classes are held. Faure began his popular cooking series years ago and all of his classes fill up quickly. He offers Romantic Dinner for Two; Parisian Bistro Cooking; French Provincial; Mediterranean; and French Baking. "The good news," Faure says smiling, "is that there is no oil, so we can add heavy cream." He adds a large dollop of cream to a perfectly blended carrot and leek soup. "We can't live without fat. But our fat should be good things – a nice butter, not McDonald's."

Sauces are Faure's specialty and he includes several in his classes. Students sit in clusters of two and four at the restaurant tables; Faure demonstrates each recipe while interjecting tips on sanitation, cooking pans and shopping tips on best buys (did you know that the Philadelphia fish market opens at 2 a.m.?). Copies of recipes are distributed and the class culminates with a candlelight meal. Classes are $40; times vary by day and season. Golden Pheasant Inn, 763 River Road, Erwinna, ☎ 610-294-9595, www.goldenpheasantinn.com.

Sand Castle Winery

Brothers Joseph and Paul Maxian, natives of Czechoslovakia, purchased 40 acres of hilltop land overlooking the Delaware River in 1974, just five years after fleeing their communist-controlled homeland. They learned about winemaking in Czechoslovakia, where their father made them work in rented vineyards for extra money. In 1985, the brothers planted their first grapevines – *Vitus vinifera*, from European stock. Then they blasted a wine cellar 30 feet into the hillside, and by 1988 finally had wine to show for their labor. Today, Sand Castle Winery's 40,000 plants yield 240,000 bottles of wine per year, and the winery has overcome the stigma of East Coast wines, earning awards nationally and internationally. An additional 32 acres of grapes have also been planted.

Sand Castle's wines were served at the Music for all Seasons opening show at Carnegie Hall in New York City.

Sand Castle Winery is open daily and holds free wine tastings. A guided tour of their vineyard and underground wine cellar is $3; the barrel tasting tour is $7.50. Special events are held throughout the year. 755 River Road, Erwinna; ☎ 800-722-9463, www.sandcastlewinery.com.

Shop Till You Drop

Solebury Township

RICE'S MARKET
Round the bend on Greenhill Road on a Tuesday at 7 a.m. and you won't believe the crowd. Thousands of people flock to Rice's, Bucks County's largest and oldest market. The outdoor event began in 1860, when Mr. A.L. Rice settled on the farm and began auctioning his products, as well as those of his neighbors, at various times of the year. Soon, farmers brought their cattle and produce for Rice to sell. By

North of New Hope

the 1950s, a market was added to the Tuesday live-stock auctions – and the 30-acre farm soon hosted more than 200 vendors from throughout the Northeast. Meander through the stalls for antiques, produce, baked goods, clothing, designer handbags, furniture and other items. Open year-round on Tuesdays, 7 a.m. to 1:30 p.m.; and from March through December on Saturdays, 7 a.m. to 1 p.m.; also open on some holidays. 6326 Greenhill Road, New Hope, ☎ 215-297-5993, www.ricesmarket.com.

Lahaska

PEDDLER'S VILLAGE

A five-mile detour off River Road, Peddler's Village is a destination in itself for shoppers. Designed to replicate an 18th-century-style village, this 42-acre shopping mecca has 75 specialty shops and restaurants, year-round festivals and craft competitions, and an antique carousel (see page 82). Open daily; extended holiday hours. At the intersection of routes 202 and 263, Lahaska; ☎ 215-794-4000, www.peddlersvillage.com.

Lumberville

THE LUMBERVILLE STORE

Think *Petticoat Junction*, or *Green Acres*. Hard to believe, but the general stores depicted in those '60s sitcoms really do still exist – in Lumberville and at other points along River Road.

Established in 1770, The Lumberville Store was used as a post office before becoming a general store in 1835. It remains one of the oldest general stores in America. Stop in for a sandwich (wonderful, though pricey) or just to peruse the antiques, jewelry, books, small-town provisions, tourist trinkets, postcards and coffee-table books. Open daily, 8 a.m. to 5 p.m. 3741 River Road, Lumberville; ☎ 215-297-5388.

Point Pleasant

POOR RICHARDS

There is absolutely no rhyme or reason to this eclectic, stuffed-with-stuff store in Point Pleasant. But that's exactly what makes the store so much fun. The experience begins on the front-lawn filled with ceramic garden fountains, benches, and flower pots; there's even a pot-belly-pig barbecue grill. Inside are rooms upon rooms of antiques, collectibles, candles, Christmas décor and items to match any mood or season. Open daily. 6 River Road, Point Pleasant; ☎ 215-297-5666.

CHACHKA GOURMET

The Eastern European word "chachka" means "something special," and this Erwinna gourmet food store is aptly named. Shelves are lined with delicacies from around the world: balsamic vinegars from France; biscotti from Italy; hot and spicy salsas; coffees and teas; chutneys; and the owners' own line of homemade "Gentleman Farmer" jams made in their 200-year-old farmhouse kitchen. Open 10 a.m. to 5 p.m. Closed Tuesdays. 905 River Road, Erwinna, ☎ 610-294-9763.

North of New Hope

Best Places to Stay

ACCOMMODATIONS PRICE SCALE
Price scale is based on a standard room for two persons, per night.
Inexpensive . . . . under $100
Moderate . . . . $100-$200
Expensive . . . . $201-$300
Deluxe . . . . more than $300

HOTEL DU VILLAGE
2535 River Road
New Hope-Solebury Township
☎ 215-862-9911, www.hotelduvillage.com
American Express and Diners Club only
Inexpensive to Moderate

Architect Morgan Colt designed this classic French restaurant (see page 97) and hotel at the turn of the 20th century. For years, the estate was used as a prep school for young women, and as part of the private Solebury School (still in existence today but at a different location). The "hotel" received its first overnight visitor in 1978 and has been entertaining guests ever since. Featured are 19 single and double rooms and family suites, all with private baths. As you may imagine, the feel is French – with wrought-iron beds, red-and-white fabrics and cozy chairs. In summer, guests may enjoy the outdoor swimming pool and tennis courts. A French-style continental breakfast is included.

HOLLYHEDGE ESTATE
6987 Upper York Road
New Hope-Solebury Township
☎ 215-862-3136 or 800-378-4496
www.hollyhedge.com
Moderate

I discovered this out-of-the-way inn when a friend had her wedding here. The 20+ acres, complete with English gardens and a natural pond, have attracted numerous brides and grooms. But the long-time-married and even the just-dating like it, too. The regal stone manor houses 15 rooms, many with fireplaces. A full breakfast is served on weekends; a continental one is offered during the week.

INN AT PHILLIPS MILL
North River Road
New Hope-Solebury Township
☎ 215-862-9919
Inexpensive to Moderate

For a truly French-country feel, this five-room, one cottage inn is perfect – if just for the opportunity to dine like royalty (see page 97) and collapse into bed. "We like people to come, stay, eat, just relax," one of the waitresses told me. And leave the kids at home.

Rooms are Parisian-size (tiny) and there's no TV or phone. A few border on gloomy, but still have a romantic charm, particularly room #2, which features a brass bed, hand-painted French dresser and a turquoise bathroom. A separate two-story stone cottage has a giant fireplace, tiled floors and lots of candles.

North of New Hope

1740 HOUSE
River Road
Lumberville
☎ 215-297-5661
Moderate

Many people adore this riverfront inn. I personally find it musty and the accommodations basic. Still, it's a good value and a nice refuge for a weekend getaway. Each of the 24 rooms has a private bath and a terrace overlooking the canal and river. Morning starts off with a buffet breakfast.

THE BLACK BASS HOTEL
3744 River Road
Lumberville
☎ 215-297-5770
www.blackbasshotel.com
Inexpensive to Moderate

The food is definitely the draw (see page 93), but there are also nine non-luxurious rooms available. It's not that the seven rooms and two suites are so terrible, but rather that (with the exception of one suite that was faux-painted 25 years ago by a local artist) none have been upgraded since the current owner bought the place – which was more than 50 years ago.

Rustic as the rooms are, four offer magnificent views of the river. "There's nothing like standing out here on the balcony, watching the sunset," one patron told me. Although the Inn refused to allow George Washington to sleep here during the Revolutionary War (the owner was loyal to the Crown), President Grover Cleveland not only slept here, but spent several weeks. Of course, the most frequent visitors are the ghosts (Revolutionary soldiers?) said to haunt the guestrooms at night.

GOLDEN PHEASANT INN
763 River Road
Erwinna
☎ 610-394-9595 or 800-830-4474
www.goldenpheasantinn.com
Inexpensive to Moderate

Originally built when canal traffic was at its peak, today's Golden Pheasant Inn is a far cry from the tavern that once catered to canal men stopping to change mules and refresh themselves with a beer. Sophisticated comfort is the theme of the Golden Pheasant's six guest rooms. "Rooms have really great beds. It's all about comfort," my hostess (one of owner Michel and Barbara Faure's five daughters) told me. And I wasn't disappointed.

There are also fireplaces, private baths, antiques, river or canal views, and a great continental breakfast. Not surprising, since French-born Chef Faure also offers one of the Delaware River Valley's greatest dining experiences (see page 98 for details).

A separate cottage with porch, kitchenette, sitting room, king-sized bed, fireplace and pullout sofa is perfect for couples, or families traveling with small children or pets (up to 40 pounds).

North of New Hope

EVERMAY ON-THE-DELAWARE
River Road, PO Box 60
Erwinna
☎ 610-294-9100
www.evermay.com
Moderate to Deluxe

The Victorian bathtub in the carriage house at the EverMay is long enough for a six-footer to stretch out and so deep that it's nearly impossible to see out.

Rumor is that the Barrymore family used to spend summers in this stately Victorian house, which was originally built in the 1700s and significantly enlarged and remodeled in the late 1800s. Listed on the National Register of Historic Places, EverMay is located between the Delaware River and Canal on 25 acres of pastures, woodlands and gardens.

We arrived just in time for tea (served daily at 4 p.m.). "These should hold you over until dinner." Our server quickly deposited a silver tray of sugar cookies, poppy bread, cucumber sandwiches and two pots of steaming tea before discreetly disappearing. The experience of sipping tea from delicate china cups in an antiques-filled parlor surrounded by oriental rugs, clocks and a grand piano takes you back in time, as do the 18 guest rooms and cottages with private baths.

All of the rooms celebrate a notable Bucks County resident (Pearl S. Buck; Colonel William Erwin, Oscar Hammerstein, Henry Mercer, David Burpee). Furnishings include walnut beds, oriental rugs, marble-topped dressers, fancy quilts and lacy pillows. Some rooms still have the original fireplaces.

Dinner is an "event" (see page 99). Breakfast is served indoors in the conservatory overlooking the gardens or, in nice weather, outdoors on the patio. The resident canine, Buddy, will likely greet you, and should you have any leftover breads or muffins (which we inevitably did), the inn's 10 sheep will be happy to share them.

Best Places to Eat

DINING PRICE SCALE
Pricing includes one entrée, with glass of wine and coffee.
Inexpensive . . . . under $20
Moderate . . . . $20-$35
Expensive . . . . over $35

American

THE BLACK BASS HOTEL
3744 River Road
Lumberville
☎ 215-297-5770
www.blackbasshotel.com
Expensive

For riverfront (and canalfront) dining, it doesn't get any better than The Black Bass. Intimate candlelit tables overlook the water. Menus are printed on brown parchment paper, reflecting the restaurant's colonial spirit. Specialties of the house include Charleston Meeting Street crab (jumbo lump crab sautéed in butter, cream, spices and cheese and baked in the oven), and coffee-lacquered duck with pear ginger chutney. Breads are fresh-baked daily

North of New Hope

The Black Bass Hotel, loyal to the Crown during the Revolutionary War, refused to allow George Washington to eat or sleep there, and in fact turned him away.

and desserts are all homemade – even the ice creams and sorbets.

The Black Bass Hotel was built in the 1740s as a tavern for rough-tough river travelers. In the early 1830s, a band of canal workers arrived at the hotel and, inadvertently, during a bar rumble, set fire to the inn. The hotel was saved from total destruction by Major Anthony Fry, who broke into the cellar and carried to safety a quantity of blasting powder that the Canal Company had stored there. The original rough-and-tumble canal bar is still downstairs, and is reportedly haunted by a ghost named Hans who was killed in the bar during a knife fight over a woman.

> ### ✕ HISTORIC TRIVIA
>
> The Black Bass served as a rural retreat for President **Grover Cleveland**, who came here to fish and find solitude.

The latest transformation of the inn occurred in 1949 when the current owner, former New Yorker Herbert Ward, purchased the hotel. British roots are strong here (Lumberville was faithful to the King during the Revolutionary War) and Mr. Ward showcases a serious collection of British memorabilia he's accumulated over the years. Included are cigar boxes, cookie tins, plates, artwork featuring British royalty, and a champagne bottle commemorating the marriage of Prince Charles and the late Princess Diana.

Herbert Ward, owner of The Black Bass Hotel, operated his first restaurant in New York City's theater district in the 1920s and '30s. Autographed photos hang on the walls, including one of the wicked witch in *The Wizard of Oz* (played by Margaret Hamilton) and of Claudette Colbert in *It Happened One Night*.

CENTRE BRIDGE INN
2998 North River Road
Solebury Township
☎ 215-862-2048
Moderate to Expensive

Pennsylvania impressionist Edward Redfield made his home in this grand house – now the home of the Centre Bridge Inn. While the beautiful house sparked Redfield's creativity, it holds a tragic history. Just like the bridge connecting Centre Bridge to Stockton, New Jersey, the inn lived through two major disasters. The first occurred in 1932, when the inn burned to the ground on Halloween night. In the late 1940s, the property was purchased by an artist living in New York City, who camped in the ruins for a summer with his wife and son. In 1952, the artist rebuilt the inn, only to have it burn again in 1959. The inn was resurrected for the last time 1961, and since then has served as a fine restaurant and perennial favorite for weddings.

The menu is extensive, with specialties such as Chilean sea bass with lemon beurre blanc sauce, and fi-

North of New Hope

As the bridge in Centre Bridge burned, impressionist Edward Redfield captured the event on canvas.

let of beef cut with fresh horseradish and an herb crust served with merlot demiglace. In summer, dining is alfresco on the terrace, overlooking the canal and river; in winter, meals are served before glowing fireplaces.

Casual Eateries

DILLY'S CORNER
Routes 32 and 263
Solebury Township
☎ 215-862-5333
Inexpensive

If it's burgers you want, look no farther than this age-old hamburger stand, located directly across the street from the Centre Bridge Inn. Hamburgers, hot dogs, french fries and soft ice cream are served, with seating largely outdoors. Don't expect a number while you wait; the theme here is playing cards. Young high school and college-aged workers hand you a card, then belt out your order according to hearts, diamonds, spades and clubs. Vegetarian burgers are available. Expect a line at the ice cream window.

French

THE INN AT PHILLIPS MILL
North River Road
Solebury Township
☎ 215-862-9919
BYOB; no credit cards
Moderate to Expensive

Even if the food was just mediocre, the dining experience would be worthy of a visit to this charming stone enclave. But fortunately, that's not the case. The French menu, featuring duck, lamb, beef and fish, is excellent and the ambience is hard to beat. First a grist mill, then a pig farm, and later, an all-girl's school, The Inn at Phillips Mill has been transformed by owner/architect Brooks Kaufman into a cozy country-French restaurant. The dining room feels more like that in a private residence, and is very romantic, with candles augmenting light from the huge, open-hearth fireplace. Ceilings are low, with dark beams; flower arrangements and gleaming copper pots appropriately add splashes of color. Although it is not luxurious, the Inn also offers five Paris-tiny rooms – perfect for an overnight.

HOTEL DU VILLAGE
2535 River Road
Solebury Township
☎ 215-862-9911
Expensive

This classic French restaurant, set high on a hill, was one of the first places I ate after moving to New Hope a decade ago, and it hasn't lost its touch. While summer dining is lovely, a candlelight winter dinner before a roaring fire is hard to beat. The *soupe à l'oignon gratinée*, as you may imagine, is superb. And specialties of the house complement the inn's warm, country-elegant feel. Although the chef changes the menu frequently, some favorites include *tournedos Henry IV* (filet, artichoke hearts and sauce béarnaise); *escalope de veau Madeira* (veal scallop, Madeira sauce and mushrooms); *civet villageois* (pastry-covered rabbit dish); and the classic *cuisses de grenouille* (frog legs, shallots, garlic, parsley, butter and cream). Crème de menthe-and-chocolate parfaits are the perfect dessert.

GOLDEN PHEASANT INN
763 River Road
Erwinna
☎ 800-830-4474 or 610-394-9595
www.goldenpheasantinn.com
Expensive

The Sunday brunch menu at the Golden Pheasant features egg dishes named after the owners' daughters and grandchildren.

I admit, I'm partial to this out-of-the-way French restaurant, since it was in the main dining room that my husband asked me to marry him. But beyond our (yes, successful) engagement dinner, the Golden Pheasant stands on its own merit. French-born chef Michel Faure and wife Barbara (along with their five now-grown daughters) have owned and operated this historic inn since 1986.

Like most of the inns along this stretch of the river, the Golden Pheasant catered to canal men who stopped to change mules and refresh themselves with a beer. Under the Faures, however, the once roughneck bar has been transformed into a sophisticated blend of colonial Bucks County and Country French (check out the huge collection of Quimper – the brightly colored pottery from Brittany).

The menu reflects Michel's classic French training (from his years at the George V, La Tour d'Argent and the Ritz in Paris). Specialties include escargots in hazelnut garlic butter, or smoked trout served with a horseradish and sour cream sauce for starters. French onion soup gratinée sets the stage for classic entrées like roasted pheasant served with apple and calvados sauce, roasted boneless duck served with sauce du jour, poached salmon served with a champagne, shrimp and lobster sauce, or roasted rack of lamb with rosemary and thyme sauce. Michel takes his sauces seriously. The wine list is extensive, featuring mostly French wines, but with some Italian and Australian thrown in. Desserts are all homemade.

☞ *DID YOU KNOW?*

Every spring, hundreds of bikers in Malcolm Forbes' **Harley Motorcycle Run** make the trip – with police escorts – from the Forbes compound in central New Jersey to the Golden Pheasant Inn for dinner.

EVERMAY ON-THE-DELAWARE
River Road, PO Box 60
Erwinna
☎ 610-924-9100
www.evermay.com
Expensive

Although the restaurant at EverMay has recently acquired a new chef, dinner does not disappoint. Served only on Friday, Saturday and Sunday nights at one seating (7:30 p.m.), dinner is in such high demand that reservations made well in advance are now necessary.

The six-course meal includes champagne and hors d'oeuvres, with a choice between two entrées and two desserts. A recent sample menu included fresh garden tomato and leek soup; local sweet corn blinis with smoked salmon; salad of frisée (also called chicory or curly endive); sautéed jumbo lump crab cake with lemon-caper-tarragon crème fraîche; or grilled tournedos of beef with portobello demiglace and sauce béarnaise; chef's cheese selection; and fresh local peaches and blueberries with fresh mint, Cointreau, and crème anglaise. Service is impeccable, delivered by white-gloved waiters. As you may expect, jackets are required.

Seafood

CUTTALOSSA INN
3498 River Road (Route 32)
Lumberville
☎ 215-297-5082
Closed Sunday
Moderate to Expensive

The Cuttalossa Inn, located about a mile south of Lumberville, is a must in summer – just for the outdoor, stone-terrace dining and view of the waterfalls and flower gardens. Built in 1833, and still in use as a stagecoach stop at the end of the 19th century, the inn (on the National Register of Historic Buildings) actually utilizes mill ruins for its outdoor dining.

A popular site for small weddings, the Cuttalossa is best known for its seafood – and especially its crab imperial, which is like a crab soufflé. Desserts (pecan and walnut pies, chocolate cakes) are all homemade by locals and the selection changes several times throughout the year.

North of New Hope A to Z

Banks

Summit Bank, 5878 Route 263, Lahaska, PA, ☎ 215-794-8801.

First Union National Bank, 5810 Easton Road, Plumsteadville, PA, ☎ 215-766-8878.

First Union, Route 611 & Stump Road, Plumsteadville, PA, ☎ 215-766-8878.

Union National Bank & Trust, 5829 Easton Road, Plumsteadville, PA, ☎ 215-766-3701.

Food Market

The Lumberville Store, 3741 River Road, Lumberville, PA, ☎ 215-297-5388.

Hospital

Hunterdon Medical Center, 2100 Westcott Drive, Flemington, NJ, ☎ 908-788-6100.

Newspapers

New Hope Gazette, 170 Old York Road, New Hope, PA, ☎ 215-862-9435.

Bucks County Courier Times, 8400 Route 13, Levittown, PA 19057, ☎ 215-949-4000.

Pharmacies

Eckerd, 5835 Easton Road, Plumsteadville, PA, ☎ 215-766-7350.

Village Pharmacy, 5770 Easton Road, Plumsteadville, PA, ☎ 215-766-8030.

Post Offices

Solebury, PA, 2997 Sugan Road, ☎ 215-297-5503.

Plumsteadville, PA, Plumsteadville Shopping Center, ☎ 215-766-7690.

Religious Services

Point Pleasant Baptist Church, 35 River Road, Point Pleasant, PA, ☎ 215-297-5047.

Carversville Christian Church, 3736 Aquetong Road, Carversville, PA, ☎ 215-297-5166.

Trinity Episcopal Church, Route 263, Solebury, PA, ☎ 215-297-5135.

Lahaska United Methodist Church, Route 263 and Street Road, Lahaska, PA, ☎ 215-794-0688.

Buckingham Friends Meeting, routes 202 & 263, Lahaska, PA, ☎ 215-794-7299.

Family of God Lutheran Church, 4770 Route 202, Buckingham, PA, ☎ 215-794-5973.

Wine & Spirits

State Liquor Store, 5837 Easton Road, Plumsteadville, PA, ☎ 215-249-2803; and 4850 Old York Road, Holicong, PA, ☎ 215-794-6800.

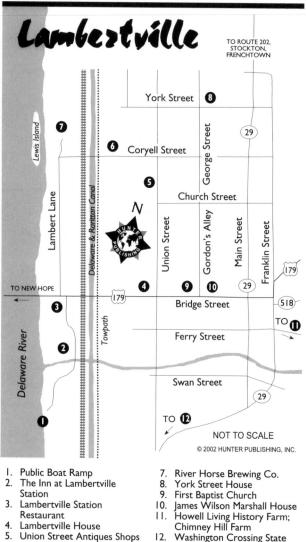

Lambertville

TO ROUTE 202, STOCKTON, FRENCHTOWN

York Street ❽

George Street
29

❼

❻ Coryell Street

Lewis Island

❺

Church Street

Lambert Lane

Delaware & Raritan Canal

N
HUNTER PUBLISHING

Union Street

Gordon's Alley

Main Street

Franklin Street

TO NEW HOPE

179

❹   ❾   ❿   29

179

Bridge Street

518

❸

TO ⓫

Towpath

Ferry Street

❷

Swan Street

29

Delaware River

❶

TO ⓬

NOT TO SCALE

© 2002 HUNTER PUBLISHING, INC.

1. Public Boat Ramp
2. The Inn at Lambertville Station
3. Lambertville Station Restaurant
4. Lambertville House
5. Union Street Antiques Shops
6. The Porkyard
7. River Horse Brewing Co.
8. York Street House
9. First Baptist Church
10. James Wilson Marshall House
11. Howell Living History Farm; Chimney Hill Farm
12. Washington Crossing State Park; Open Air Theater

Lambertville

Once a laid-back, sleepy river town, New Jersey's Lambertville has been transformed in recent years, sprouting new restaurants, inns and shops at a record pace. The growth is not surprising. Given the bustling popularity of New Hope, just across the bridge, it seems only natural that businesses from the artist enclave would simply spill across the river. However, Lambertville's revitalization has more to do with the Delaware River – and its shad – than with artisans.

History

Like New Hope, Lambertville (colonized in 1705) grew into an industrial center, with the Delaware River as its backdrop. The prosperity and development of the town was largely due to the efforts of its first settler, **John Holcombe**, who lobbied hard to have York Road, the main road from Philadelphia to New York, go through Lambertville. Originally, the road was planned to pass north of there, in what is now Stockton.

✕ HISTORIC TRIVIA

Lambertville and New Hope, directly across the Delaware from one another, were once a single town called **Coryell's Ferry** (named after the man who operated the boat).

A Center of Industry

New Hope and Lambertville once printed their own currency.

By the mid-1800s Lambertville was a thriving industrial center. In 1859, the **Lambertville Iron Works** was established and, for years, the **Kooker Sausage Company** thrived in what is today appropriately called the **Porkyard**, an antiques center. At the height of its productivity, Lambertville employed 3,000 factory workers, turning out such products as wooden wagon wheels, rubber boots and shoes, bottled beer, railway cars and locomotives, ceramics and the first hairpins.

The 19th & 20th Centuries

The railroad also brought prosperity, with Lambertville's station serving as a hub of activity. The two-and-a-half-story stone train station was initially the headquarters of the **Belvidere Delaware Railroad**, serving passengers on the local lines from Belvidere to Trenton. In the late 1800s, the Pennsylvania Railroad took over the line and instituted service to New England. The rail's glory was short lived, however, and by the middle of the 20th century the railroad was closed, as were many of Lambertville's industries, which had relocated to urban areas.

At a time when the Impressionist artists kept New Hope alive and vibrant, Lambertville experienced a prolonged economic slump that lasted for decades. It was not until the late 1970s to early '80s – when federal and citizens' groups cleaned up the Delaware River and the shad began to run again – that Lambertville's businesses began to boom once more.

Business entrepreneur **Dan Whitaker** was first on board with the purchase of the old Pennsylvania-Belvidere Railroad headquarters. Whitaker converted the station into the town's first major restaurant, The Lambertville Station, and five years later added the 45-room Inn at Lambertville Station, overlooking the Delaware River (see pages 122 and 127 for details). Soon, other business owners started fixing up their buildings and new investors came to town. Artisans, upscale antiques shops and galleries followed, slowly at first and then in a steady stream. With them came an explosion of top-notch restaurants.

Despite its upscale revival, Lambertville (population 4,000) maintains its hometown feel. Victorian and brick Federal row houses, now newly polished and painted, look much as they did in their heyday. Gardens bloom and streets are lined with trees. Surprisingly, tourism has not suffocated the town's neighborhood feel.

Lambertville

Sunup to Sundown

Walks & Tours

Delaware & Raritan Canal State Park

A public boat launch is located a half-mile south of The Inn at Lambertville Station.

The Delaware & Raritan Canal State Park runs through the heart of Lambertville, offering opportunities for walking, jogging, biking, and – in snowy winters – cross-country skiing. The Canal Commission recently restored the canal walls and towpath in Lambertville, further improving an already wonderful recreational area.

On the second Sunday of each month, the park offers free, guided canal walks. These informative walks along the towpath leave at 10 a.m. from the Lambertville lock. (You can reach the lock by taking the towpath south from Cavallo Park at the foot of Union Street, or by following the gravel road behind The Inn at Lambertville Station to its end at the water treatment plant.) For more information, contact the Delaware & Raritan Canal Commission, ☎ 732-873-3050.

Town Walks

Lambertville-New Hope Walks offers a 90-minute journey that takes walkers through two towns, in two states, down quaint streets and along the canal as a guide relays the strange, bizarre, fascinating tales of two cities – New Hope, Pennsylvania and Lambertville, New Jersey. Groups meet on Friday and Saturday nights at 8 p.m. and on Sunday afternoons at 3 p.m. at the Lambertville Station; the cost is $8 adult; $6 children under 15; children under five are free.

RIVER HORSE BREWERY TOUR

Founded in 1994, the River Horse Brewing Company is located in Lambertville's former OTC Cracker Factory. All production takes place at this facility – from brewing to packaging. River Horse is the area's only microbrewery, and offers walking tours of the kegging and bottling operations. The brewery also has a tasting room and retail shop, and is open daily for tours and samples from noon to 5 p.m. 80 Lambert Lane, ☎ 609-397-7776.

Another tour given by the company takes you through Lambertville and New Hope's old red-light districts, with stops at pubs and taverns. Tales of presidents, senators, brothels, authors, speakeasies, and ghosts are shared. Must be 21 or older. Tours meet at the Lambertville Station, Tuesday and Wednesday nights, at 8 p.m., and cost $8. Lambertville-New Hope Walks, ☎ 609-397-1898, www.LambertvilleNewHopeWalks.com.

If a self-guided tour is more your style, pick up a map from Lambertville Trading Company, Sojourner, Coryell Gallery or The Mercantile (see pages 114-118) and view the town's most outstanding period architecture at your own pace. The walk, which takes about 45 minutes, begins at the Marshall House (see page 111) and ends in the center of town. More than 20 buildings are highlighted on the tour.

Lambertville

Horse-Drawn Carriage Rides

New Hope-based **Bucks County Carriages** provides services across the Delaware river in Lambertville. Horse-drawn carriage rides begin at the Lambertville Station and meander through town; the cost is $12 for adults and $6 for children. Riding horses are also available for escorted trail rides and lessons. 2586 North River Road, New Hope. ☎ 215-862-3582.

Historic Sites

James Wilson Marshall House & Museum

The man who is credited with starting the 1849 California Gold Rush, James Marshall, grew up in this 2½-story Federal-style brick home, which was built by his father in 1816. Marshall lived in the house from the time he was six years old until age 21, when he packed his carpentry tools and headed west to California. In 1848, the Lambertville native found gold. News did not reach the east coast and other parts of the world until a year later, triggering the Gold Rush of '49. Even though Marshall found the gold by accident and died a pauper, he is held in high esteem in Lambertville.

Don't miss "Are We There Yet? Gil's Journey Upstream," an exhibit at the Marshall House Museum that chronicles the history and significance of shad fishing on the Delaware River.

✖ HISTORIC TRIVIA

Lambertville's **James Marshall** discovered gold in 1848 while building a sawmill near Sacramento, CA. He described the nugget as "half the size and shape of a pea. It made my heart thump," he later wrote, "for I was certain it was gold." The cornerstone of the **First Baptist Church** on Bridge Street contains nuggets of gold from Marshall's famous discovery.

The Marshall House was saved from demolition in 1964 and is owned today by the State of New Jersey. The house is listed on both the state and national

Lambertville

registers of historic places and is leased to the Lambertville Historical Society as a museum and meeting place. The museum is furnished according to an 1834 household inventory, and displays photographs, maps and artifacts showing life in early Lambertville. Open April through October, Saturdays and Sundays, from 1 to 4 p.m.; admission is free. 62 Bridge Street, ☎ 609-397-0770.

Howell Living History Farm

Howell Living History Farm, just south of Lambertville, has been worked for more than 250 years.

Located south of Lambertville, the Howell Living History Farm provides a perfect outing for families. Restored in 1984 to its 1900-1910 appearance, the farm enables visitors to experience hands-on, turn-of-the-century farming. Observe horses, cows, sheep and pigs, and try your hand at ice harvesting, maple sugaring, sleigh rides, beekeeping, honey harvesting, hogslopping, fiddlin', and other farm-related events. The farm is open weekends, February through November, 10 a.m. to 4 p.m.; admission is free. Valley Road (two miles south of Lambertville), ☎ 609-737-3299, www.howellfarm.com.

Recreation

Shad Fishing on the Delaware

 Shad is sacred in Lambertville, and visitors can anticipate great shad fishing in April. Guides from **New Hope Fly Fishing** will gladly take you out on the river for half- or full-day trips. ☎ 215-862-6896, www.flyfishnewhopepa.com.

Shad lovers shouldn't miss the town's annual **Shad Festival** (see page 18).

Hot-Air Ballooning

Lambertville and the surrounding Delaware River Valley are hotbeds for ballooning. Traditional packages include an hour-long flight, champagne and hors d'oeuvres, and are $160 per person. An exclusive two-person flight reserves the entire balloon just for the two of you for $390. Contact **Alexandria Balloon Flights**, 93 Hickory Corner Road, Milford; ☎ 888-HOT-AIR-7, or 908-479-4878.

Arts & Theater

Performing Arts

Riverside Symphonia

♪♫♪ The creation of Riverside Symphonia more than a decade ago gave tiny Lambertville its own professional orchestra dedicated to providing world-class music. The orchestra has become a vibrant part of the cultural life of the community; concerts, presented throughout the year at Saint John the Evangelist church in Lambertville, feature distinguished guest performers and conductors. Ticket prices range from $19 to $32; contact the box office for schedule or reservations at ☎ 609-397-7300 or 215-862-3300, www.riversidesymphonia.org.

Lambertville

Washington Crossing Open Air Theater

Nestled deep in the forest of New Jersey's Washington Crossing State Park (just a few miles south of Lambertville), this summer-only theater has delighted locals for years. The theater, as its name suggests, is "open-air," meaning that a sudden rainstorm can result in a cancellation or an early curtain call. Shows are presented by local community theater groups, and are family-friendly, such as *Annie*, *The Sound of Music*, *Brigadoon*, and *South Pacific*. Gates open at 7:15 p.m. and the outdoor amphitheater-style bench seats are on a first-come, first-served basis. Light refreshments are sold, but many people arrive early and bring their own picnic suppers. The season runs from May 30 through the end of August; tickets are $7.50. Washington Crossing State Park, 355 Washington Crossing-Pennington Road, Titusville, ☎ 609-737-1826.

Shop Till You Drop

Antiques & Art

Union Street

Even when Lambertville's People's Store on Union Street closed as a local department store and reopened with three floors of antiques, no one expected to see most of Union Street's shops filled with art and antiques. Not only did that happen, but Lambertville has become one of the most important and respected centers for antiques and art in the north-eastern US. The only way to truly experience the scope of the arts and antiquities here is to stroll in and out of the many galleries, but the following shops should not be missed.

ANTIQUES CENTER AT THE PEOPLE'S STORE

This is the store where the area's thriving antiques market began. The converted People's Store, a 40-shop antiques cooperative, is Lambertville's oldest and largest affordable antiques center. If you're like me, you won't leave empty-handed. Open daily from 10 a.m. to 6 p.m. Corner of Church and Union streets, ☎ 609-397-9808.

AMERICA ANTIQUES & DESIGN

A circa-1911 brick garage and former dance hall provides the backdrop for this eclectic collection of 19th- and 20th-century artifacts, paintings, furniture and architectural iron. A combination of high-style, high-design and emerging concepts, America features five showrooms on two floors. It takes a bold eye to combine 1940s French furniture with a Chinese black-lacquered table, 1960s nickel-plated deco floor lamp and heavily carved Chippendale mirror from 1885 all in one room – but owner Cheryl Campbell has been successfully nurturing this style for years. Her clientele includes the Ralph Lauren design company and the J. Peterman Corporation. Open daily. 5 South Main Street, ☎ 609-397-6966.

BEST OF FRANCE ANTIQUES

I absolutely adore this store. Gilded pieces blend with bronze and marble sculpture and Louis XV furniture. When my daughter was very young, we used to pretend we lived in this high-ceilinged Parisian palace, moving from room to room, viewing beds, dining room tables, the outside garden and iron work. Best of France is a must-see. It is also the area's largest direct importer of antique furniture and sculpture from France. Open daily. 204 North Union Street, ☎ 609-397-9881.

GOLDEN NUGGET ANTIQUE FLEA MARKET

Located just south of Lambertville on Route 29, the Golden Nugget Antique Flea Market is one of the finest on the East Coast. Be sure to get there early. The market features 40 inside shops and 250 outdoor tables. Open year-round, Wednesdays, Saturdays and Sundays, 8 a.m. to 4 p.m; ☎ 609-397-0811.

THE PORKYARD

Once the location of the Kooker Sausage Company, the Porkyard now houses two art-and-antiques shops. **Porkyard Antiques**, ☎ 609-397-2088, carries country antiques (furniture, lamps, quilts, decoys) and fine artwork. **The Coryell Gallery at the Porkyard**, ☎ 609-397-0804, represents prominent Delaware River Valley artists with oils, watercolors, prints, sculpture and pottery. Located at 8 Coryell Street, the Porkyard is open Wednesday through Sunday, 11 a.m. to 5 p.m.

Fine Art Reproductions

HOWARD MANN ART CENTER

A Lambertville classic, The Howard Mann Art Center has been coined "the supermarket of fine art." It has more than 15,000 square feet of space, featuring high-end reproductions of Chagall, Picasso, Rembrandt, Goya, Dali, Whistler, and others. Open Wednesday through Sunday. 45 North Main Street, ☎ 609-397-2300.

Specialty Shops

Aside from arts and antiques, Lambertville offers a number of interesting specialty shops and boutiques, many selling unique wares from around the world. Most stores are one-of-a-kind and independently owned and operated. Again, the best way to experience them is to stroll in and out, but the following shouldn't be missed.

SOJOURNER
Annual buying trips to Indonesia, Turkey, Guatemala, Ecuador and Peru keep this eclectic store filled with fabulous masks, textiles, clothing, loose beads, jewelry and instruments. Open daily. 26 Bridge Street, ☎ 609-397-8849.

An early 19th-century hand-carved marble Buddha from Tibet is one of the many finds at Sojourner.

BLUE RACCOON
Housed in a former bakery, Blue Raccoon defines itself as "new country" specializing in terrific furniture, gifts and accessories. The store has graced the covers of *Victoria* magazine and *Philadelphia Magazine*, among others. Look for slipcovered sofas and feel-good leather chairs while you listen to their signature finger-snapping jazz. Of course, no visit to Blue Raccoon is complete without seeing Dottie and Dash, their English bulldogs who double as models. Open daily. 6 Coryell Street (in the Porkyard), ☎ 800-452-0098, www.blueraccoon.com.

Lambertville

THE URBAN ARCHAEOLOGIST
Every piece inside this elegant store is hand-picked from Greece and Italy. Offerings include dinnerware, handblown glassware, ancient and modern jewelry, unique lighting fixtures, imported art pieces, garden and landscaping items and furniture. Open daily. 63 Bridge Street, ☎ 609-397-9588.

ALMIRAH
India native Prasanna Sawant and wife Sarah travel to India several times a year for the furnishings that appear in this colorful shop. They specialize in Colonial Indian furniture and accessories. Bold, beautiful fabrics blend with paper star lanterns, teak and rosewood furniture, and dupatts – garments worn by women in India as scarves. Open Thursday through Sunday. 53 North Union Street, ☎ 609-397-6100.

CELT-IBERIA TRADERS
This gallery-store features imported handcrafted gifts, home décor, jewelry and accessories from Ireland and Spain. 9 South Main Street, ☎ 609-773-0180.

After Dark

While there are no wild nightclubs in Lambertville, that's not to say there is no nightlife. Several bars routinely host live performers, and restaurants stay open late. Evening carriage rides are a favorite activity for visitors. The following are among the notable night attractions.

THE BOAT HOUSE
Nestled inside the Porkyard near Hamilton's Grill, this tiny, two-story bar is a longtime favorite drinking spot in Lambertville, and perfect for a cocktail before or after dinner. Boating memorabilia – paintings, photos, oars, fishing rods and the like – hang from the walls and ceilings. A narrow stairway leads to a tiny loft where you can sink into a couch or sit in a high-back chair. 8½ Coryell Street, ☎ 609-397-2244.

LEFT BANK LIBATIONS
A luxury hotel bar located in Lambertville House (see page 121), Left Bank Libations features a cozy 32-seat lounge plus an additional 24 seats outside on the front porch of the hotel. Every Friday is jazz night, featuring a jazz duo from 6 to 11 p.m. 32 Bridge Street, ☎ 609-397-0200.

Lambertville House's Left Bank Libations is one of the only non-smoking bars in New Jersey.

THE SWAN
This is one of Lambertville's most historic restaurant/pubs. In warm weather, drinks are served in the restaurant's beautiful cobblestone courtyard. Exceptional light fare is available. 43 South Main Street, ☎ 609-397-3552.

MITCHELL'S CAFE
Owned by the same family for more than 30 years, Mitchell's Café is a neighborhood bar with a country & western flavor. Every first and third Wednesday, however, the C&W feel gives way to Mitchell's famous Irish session – with singers, pipers and dancers in full blast. A variety of beers and ales are on tap, and at least one single malt is offered. 11½ Church Street, ☎ 609-397-9853.

Lambertville

THE STATION PUB
Located on the lower level beneath the Lambertville Station restaurant, The Station Pub is decorated with photographs of jazz musicians. On weekends, live jazz and blues are played here. 11 Bridge Street, at The Lambertville Station restaurant, ☎ 609-397-8300.

Best Places to Stay

ACCOMMODATIONS PRICE SCALE	
Price scale is based on a standard room for two persons, per night.	
Inexpensive	under $100
Moderate	$100-$200
Expensive	$201-$300
Deluxe	more than $300

YORK STREET HOUSE BED & BREAKFAST
42 York Street
☎ 609-397-3007
www.yorkstreethouse.com
Moderate to Expensive

Over the years, the York Street House Bed & Breakfast has served as a private residence, church and boarding house.

Known locally as Massey Mansion, the York Street House Bed & Breakfast was originally built in 1909 by George Massey as a 25th wedding anniversary gift for his wife. Massey commissioned two well-known Philadelphia architects to design a suburban home that would incorporate modern design elements. The result – gas and electric lighting, central heating and a central vacuum system (still in the basement today) – earned the house a feature in the 1911 issue of *House & Garden* magazine.

Original artful touches remain, including a stained glass window in the dining room, and fireplaces surrounded by tiles from the Moravian Pottery & Tile Works in nearby Doylestown (see page 166).

In 1983, the house was renovated and opened as York Street House Bed & Breakfast. Now under the care of Mark and Laurie Weinstein, the house's grandeur continues, with special attention paid to women traveling alone.

In the dining room, a large selection of teas, coffee (freshly ground and brewed) and home-baked cookies are always available. Breakfast (full) is served by candlelight, and all rooms have private baths, down comforters, fireplaces, signature soaps and bathrobes.

LAMBERTVILLE HOUSE
32 Bridge Street
☎ 609-397-0200 or 888-867-8859
www.lambertvillehouse.com
Expensive

Once Lambertville's first post office, Lambert's Inn (as it was called in 1812) served as a stagecoach stop for dignitaries, business leaders and US presidents traveling between New York City and Philadelphia.

More than a century later, in the 1980s, the hotel fell victim to real estate speculation and neglect, and the property sat vacant for over a decade before being purchased by Bucks County developer George Michel, who spent three years and $3.5 million to restore the hotel to its original 19th-century grandeur.

Lambertville

Mr. Michel was able to save the first floor foyer and staircase, exposed stone walls and fireplaces.

The hotel reopened in 1997. Now listed on the National Register of Historic Places, Lambertville House offers 26 large guest rooms and suites furnished with elegant antiques and reproductions of classic furniture and fabrics. Most of the rooms have fireplaces and Jacuzzis, with balconies overlooking a beautifully landscaped courtyard. Health club access and horse-drawn carriage rides (seasonal) are available.

THE INN AT LAMBERTVILLE STATION
The Lambertville Waterfront
11 Bridge Street
☎ 609-397-8300
www.lambertvillestation.com
Moderate to Expensive

The Lambertville railway station was designed by architect Thomas Ustick Walter, who also designed the dome of the US Capitol in Washington DC.

Built in 1985 as an adjunct to the then-newly-restored Lambertville Station restaurant, The Inn at Lambertville Station offers 45 rooms filled with antiques, featuring décor inspired by great cities around the world: Paris, San Francisco, London, New Orleans, etc., each offering river views. An honor bar in the lobby is the perfect place for a drink and to unwind after a day of walking. Continental breakfast arrives with a morning newspaper.

CHIMNEY HILL FARM INN
207 Goat Hill Road
☎ 609-397-1516 or 800-211-INNS (4667)
Moderate to Expensive
www.chimneyhillinn.com

You'll need a car to get to this inn, which is located just south of Lambertville. But once you're there,

your car may never move. This 1820 fieldstone structure has been heralded by *Colonial Homes* and *Philadelphia Magazine* as the perfect getaway, and it's
the type of place where you hang up the "do not dis-
turb" sign and disappear.

The grounds of this country estate occupy a site very
near to where George Washington surveyed the Delaware during the bitter winter of 1776. Now serving
as a secluded country inn, Chimney Hill Farm –
scattered across eight acres – features a sunken garden cottage, eight canopy-bedded rooms in the
house's gabled wings (added in 1927), and four barn
suites. The elegant living room features oriental
rugs, wide-plank wood floors, a fireplace and baby
grand piano. Breakfast, served in front of the fireplace, is superb.

Best Places to Eat

Lambertville may be tiny in size (just one mile long),
but it is "el grande" in flavor. You want French food?
Thai? Seafood cooked on an open grill? Sushi? Ca-
jun? Italian? Lambertville's got it.

DINING PRICE SCALE
Pricing includes one entrée, with *glass of wine and coffee.*
Inexpensive . . . . under $20
Moderate. . . . . $20-$35
Expensive. . . . . over $35

Lambertville

American

ANTON'S AT THE SWAN

43 South Main Street
☎ 609-397-1960
www.antonsattheswan.com
Moderate to Expensive

Many of Lambertville's restaurants are tiny and expect you to BYOB.

Anton Dodel purchased this former hotel in 1990 and, that same year, Anton's at the Swan was named one of the 10 best restaurants by *The New York Times*. It is now a well-established Lambertville favorite. Anton's continues to earn high marks with eclectic fare like sautéed lobster with apples and braised fennel, and roasted pork with persimmons and wild mushrooms.

Anton makes his own butter ("fresher than the norm"), and desserts, as you may expect, are decadent. There's always something chocolate on the menu, and usually a flan as well.

★ CULINARY SECRET

The **Lambertville Trading Company** had the first cappuccino bar in the region, and still serves great coffee, cappuccino and biscotti. 43 Bridge Street, ☎ 609-397-2232. Open daily.

HAMILTON'S GRILL ROOM
8 Coryell Street
☎ 609-397-4343
www.hamiltonsgrillroom.com
BYOB
Expensive

This out-of-the-way, open-grill restaurant is quite possibly the best in the entire Delaware River Valley. Owner Jim Hamilton grew up in Lambertville and built his career creating Broadway sets. Traveling through the Mediterranean countryside ultimately led him to an exploration of food and flavors, and Hamilton soon sought out opportunities to cook with great chefs like Alain Saillac, Jasper White, Jeremiah Tower and Jacques Pepin. In 1988, he returned to his hometown to open the now-renowned restaurant.

A huge charcoal grill serves as the restaurant's centerpiece, and diners in the Grill Room can sit at the bar and chat with executive chef Mark Miller as he turns out expertly cooked fish and meats. Shrimp with anchovy butter and rib-eye steak are house specialties, as is the signature grappa torte with grapes. There are three indoor dining rooms, but dine outdoors if possible. Tables covered with white linen and set around a courtyard fountain next to the canal make this by far the venue of choice for summer dining.

The Bishop Room at Hamilton's Grill displays a striking reproduction of Edouard Manet's "Luncheon in the Grass." The restaurant's Gallery Room showcases a painting of a 10-by-10-foot nude.

Lambertville

FROM BROADWAY TO BISTROS

Former theatrical set designer **Jim Hamilton** left Broadway to design (and run) restaurants in his hometown of Lambertville. Hamilton started his new career with an addition to the Swan Hotel, then opened Hamilton's Grill Room. In 2000, he took on another Lambertville restaurant, The Fish House (see page 130). On Broadway, Hamilton's first set design was for *The Subject Was Roses*, starring then-newcomer Martin Sheen. Other credits include *Irma La Douce*, *The World of Suzy Wong*, *The King and I* and *Destry Rides Again*.

Breakfast & Lunch

FULL MOON RESTAURANT
23 Bridge Street
☎ 609-397-1096
No credit cards
Inexpensive

Open for breakfast and lunch only, this '80s-era (actually established in 1979) art-deco-style eatery is always packed, for good reason. Blackboard specials feature omelets (try the avocado, salsa and cheddar), entrées (such as baked artichokes), sandwiches (jerk chicken is a favorite) and homemade soups. Portions are huge so you may want to share. Décor is fun – lush green plants, vaulted ceilings and bubbling fish tanks.

> ★ **CULINARY SECRET**
>
> **The Church Street Bistro** makes a mean Bloody Mary. 11½ Church Street; closed Monday and Tuesday. ☎ 609-397-4383.

Eclectic

THE LAMBERTVILLE STATION
11 Bridge Street
☎ 609-397-8300
www.lambertvillestation.com
Moderate to Expensive

After years of decline, the Pennsylvania-Belvidere station headquarters was purchased, painstakingly restored and transformed into a restaurant. The massive exterior was returned to its original beauty. The interior, with its etched glass, polished oak, gleaming brass and antiques, reflects a combination of past and present. The menu is eclectic, featuring rare finds such as wild game and alligator chili. The specialty of the house is a seafood crêpe.

The Lambertville Station sells take-home portions of its popular homemade coconut bread and honey-mustard salad dressing.

French

MANON
19 North Union Street
☎ 609-397-2596
BYOB; no credit cards
Moderate to Expensive

A friend reluctantly introduced me to this tiny Provençal French eatery, after which she begged me not

Lambertville

to tell. But the food and ambience (sponge-painted walls, sunflowers everywhere, a ceiling reminiscent of Van Gogh's "Starry Night") are just too exceptional to bypass. Outside, the restaurant is painted in the bright saffron-yellow and deep-blue color scheme typical of Provence. Inside, the food reflects that served in the typical French home.

While owner/chef Michel Dumas, originally from Arles, trained at La Bonne Auberge in Antibes and l'Oustau de Beaumanière in Les Baux de Provence, his cuisine isn't at all French haute. Crisp breads, olive oil and olives are a prologue to French classics such as *le filet de boeuf au roquefort* (filet of beef with roquefort sauce), *le carré d'agneau à la fleur de thym* (rack of lamb with thyme crust), and *le foie de veau aux échalotes confites au miel sauce bercy* (calf liver with a honey-shallot confit in butter and wine sauce). The warm goat cheese salad is delicious, as are the homemade desserts.

Italian

DeANNA'S
18 South Main Street (corner of Main and Lilly streets)
☎ 609-397-8957
BYOB; no credit cards
Moderate

Owner DeAnna learned how to make her regional Italian dishes from her grandparents and still makes all of her food individually to order. Choose from specialties like Sicilian meat loaf, homemade pasta with sundried tomatoes and pinenut cream sauce, and vegetable lasagna, with DeAnna's famous ricotta cheesecake for dessert. Expect a wait as the restaurant is tiny – just two rooms. Dining in the lovely garden is also an option.

⭐ **CULINARY SECRET**

Giuseppe's garlic pizza with red sauce is a must for garlic lovers; the cannoli is also excellent. Corner of Bridge and Union streets. Open daily; no credit cards. ☎ 609-397-1500.

BELL'S UNION STREET RESTAURANT
183 North Union Street
☎ 609-397-2226
No credit cards
Inexpensive

A decade ago, when I lived in New Hope, Bell's had the cheapest Italian food in town. It still does. The menu remains basic, filled with Italian war-horse pasta dishes like carbonara, marinara, pesto and Alfredo. The crowd is mostly locals, as Bell's sits plop in the middle of a residential neighborhood. Don't expect fancy; the floor is linoleum and chairs are plain wood, but the prices are low. Pastas range from $7 for spaghetti with oil and garlic to $10 for tortellini in a cream sauce with peas and prosciutto. A charcoal-grilled boneless rib-eye steak with fries and salad is only $13.

Lambertville

Seafood

THE FISH HOUSE
2 Canal Street
☎ 609-397-6477
BYOB
Moderate

Jim Hamilton's second Lambertville venture, The Fish House, is home to a retail fish market as well as a restaurant. Hamilton himself designed the attractive two-story space which once served as a warehouse. Visitors are welcomed through a pair of wide, arching glass and wood warehouse doors. Inside is the fish market, and a two-story wall of water falling over stainless steel panels shaped to resemble fish scales.

A raw bar offers an ever-changing selection of oysters, and the shucker is both informative and fun to watch. Fish selections, as you may imagine, are diverse, but there are a few red-meat selections available for the non-seafood lover. The kitchen is open and located smack in the center of the restaurant.

Thai

SIAM
61 North Main Street
☎ 609-397-8128
BYOB; no credit cards
Inexpensive

The only disappointment about this popular Thai restaurant is that you may not get a table. Locals have staked their claim, so without a reservation, expect a long wait for authentic dishes such as crispy whole fish (yes, with the eyes still intact); mee krob (crispy rice vermicelli noodles with shrimp and ground pork) served only at lunch according to Thailand tradition, and sticky rice with coconut milk.

Lambertville A to Z

Animal Hospital

Lambertville Animal Clinic, 66 York Street, Lambertville, NJ, ☎ 609-397-3657.

Banks

First Union National Bank, 31 Bridge Street, ☎ 609-397-0047.

Main Street Bank, 39 Bridge Street, ☎ 609-397-6090.

United Trust, 333 North Main Street, ☎ 609-397-6020.

Farm Market

Homestead Farm Market, 262 North Main Street, ☎ 609-397-8285.

Lambertville

Gas Stations

Exxon Heath's Service, 83 Bridge Street, ☎ 609-397-0433.

Cifelli's Sunoco, Inc., 82 Bridge Street, ☎ 609-397-1212.

Health Club

Center Club at Lambertville, 80 Lambertville Lane, ☎ 609-397-8900.

Hospital

Hunterdon Medical Center, 2100 Westcott Drive, Flemington, NJ, ☎ 908-788-6100.

Movie Theater

Cinema Plaza, 240 US Highway 202 & 31, Flemington, NJ, ☎ 908-782-2777.

Newspapers

Hunterdon County Democrat, 18 Minneakoning Road, Flemington, NJ, ☎ 908-782-4747.

The Beacon, PO Box 8, Hopewell, NJ, ☎ 609-466-1190.

Pharmacies

Bear Apothecary Shoppe, 9 North Union Street, ☎ 609-397-1351.

Lambertville Pharmacy, 1 Cherry Street, ☎ 609-397-0730.

Post Office

Lambertville, 10 York Street, ☎ 609-397-0061.

Religious Services

Centenary United Methodist Church, 108 Union Street, ☎ 609-397-2468.

First Baptist Church, 57 Bridge Street, ☎ 609-397-0547.

First Presbyterian Church, 31 North Union Street, ☎ 609-397-0650.

Kingdom Hall Jehovah's Witnesses, Rocktown Road, ☎ 609-397-3646.

Mt. Carmel Baptist Church, 247 North Main Street, ☎ 609-397-9814.

Old Rocks Community Church, 236 Rocktown-Lambertville Road, ☎ 609-397-8916.

St. Andrew's Church, Main & York Streets, ☎ 609-397-0194.

St. John the Evangelist Church, 44 Bridge Street, ☎ 609-397-3350.

Lambertville

Second English Presbyterian Church of Amwell at Mt. Airy, 37 Mount Airy Village Road, ☎ 609- 397-2086.

Wine & Spirits

Tomasello Winery Inc., (retail showroom), 1 North Union Street, ☎ 609-397-5577.

Walker's Wine and Spirits, 86 Bridge Street, ☎ 609-397-0625.

Welsh's Wines, 8 South Union Street, ☎ 609-397-8243.

North of Lambertville

Sergeantsville, Rosemont, Stockton and Frenchtown

*A*lthough the New Jersey side of the Delaware is not initially as scenic as Pennsylvania's River Road, it holds many artistic treasures and is worthy of exploration. While this chapter focuses primarily on Route 29, it does take a few detours along the way.

Overview

Stockton

Begin in Lambertville and head north on Route 29 to the first "country" town of Stockton, population 686. Like much of the region, Stockton's life centered around the river, mostly on the ferry operated by Colonel John Reading. One of the region's first inhabitants, Reading was one of the men chosen to meet with Native American Indians to purchase land. Reading chose a large tract bordering the Delaware River – part of which included the present-day Stockton. He also played a major role in the planning of the proposed York Road, which was to serve as the major artery connecting Philadelphia

North of Lambertville

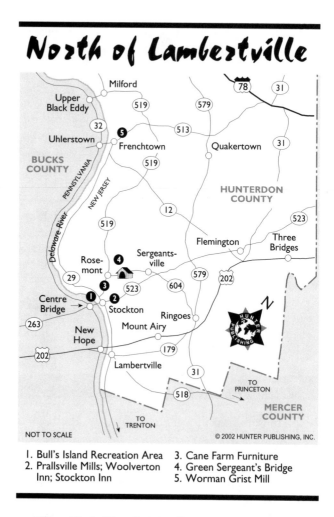

1. Bull's Island Recreation Area
2. Prallsville Mills; Woolverton Inn; Stockton Inn
3. Cane Farm Furniture
4. Green Sergeant's Bridge
5. Worman Grist Mill

and New York City. Originally, the road was to pass straight through Readings Ferry (as Stockton was then called). But intense lobbying downstream resulted in a rerouting of York Road through Lambertville. When Colonel Reading died in 1717, the ferry ceased operation and the town – no longer on the main thoroughfare – never regained its early importance.

In 1794, **John Prall, Jr.**, a veteran of the Revolutionary War, purchased property containing a quarry, where he built a grist mill, a sawmill, an oil mill and several stone dwellings. That area became known as **Prallsville** (the Prallsville Mills remain today).

☞ **DID YOU KNOW?**

Stockton's native son John Deats, an inventor, gave farmers the Deats plow and the Deats corn sheller.

A covered wooden bridge was constructed across the Delaware in 1814, connecting the settlements on both sides of the river; at that time both were called Centre Bridge. In 1832, while the canal was being dug, Centre Bridge came alive with canal workers, many of whom were Irish immigrants, creating a need for food, lodging and supplies. One resident turned his home into a hotel, and a schoolhouse was built on the spot where the Stockton Elementary School now stands.

Many buildings in New York City are made from stone quarried in the Stockton area.

In 1850 the railroad came through, and three years later, a new post office was built near the bridge. Centre Bridge (on the Jersey side) was renamed Stockton in honor of **Senator Robert Field Stockton** who helped make the canal a reality.

BRIDGE WOES

During a flood in 1841, the covered bridge at Centre Bridge broke into two and struck the Lambertville Bridge on its way downstream.

On July 22, 1923, lightning struck the wooden covered bridge and set it on fire. Fire brigades from New Hope and Lambertville helped to battle the blaze, but the bridge was destroyed. The citizens of Stockton and Centre Bridge went without a bridge for nearly four years, before the current steel bridge was erected.

The Stockton of today appears much as it did in the 18th century. There is no industry, not even a bank, although there is now a handful of restaurants and shops. Brightly painted clapboard houses dot Main Street, culminating at the historic **Stockton Inn** (made famous by composer Richard Rodgers).

★ FAMOUS FACES

Richard Rodgers was staying in the Stockton Inn when he wrote the tune *There's A Small Hotel*, from the Broadway show *On Your Toes*.

Sergeantsville

From Stockton, Route 29 follows the river, but for this tour bear right onto Route 523 to Sergeantsville shortly after passing the Stockton Inn. This detour, with its rolling hills and still-pastoral fields, gives a feel for Hunterdon County's deep-rooted agricultural tradition. Also settled in 1700, Sergeantsville was once the center of a massive peach industry. In 1850 a physician planted 3,000 peach trees, and by the 1860s his trees were bearing fruit, which was being shipped by rail to New York. Peach growing stimulated other local industries, such as basket making, and employed hundreds of people. By the turn of the century, however, the San Jose scale appeared in Hunterdon County and nearly wiped out the industry. By 1959, Hunterdon County's two million peach trees had diminished to just 15,000. Today, the town is home to the wonderful Sergeantsville Inn (see page 156).

North of Lambertville

In a single day in 1882 more than 64 carloads of peaches were shipped from Sergeantsville to New York.

Rosemont

Traveling west on **Rosemont-Ringoes Road** from Sergeantsville, you will go through New Jersey's last remaining covered bridge, Green Sergeant's Bridge (see page 141), to the village of Rosemont, highlighted by a country store and Cane Farm Furniture (see page 144).

Frenchtown

From Rosemont, return to Route 29 and head north along the river to Frenchtown. This surprise-filled river town took root in 1794 when Swiss immigrant **Paul Henri Mallet-Prevost** came to America after fleeing a French order for his arrest. Prevost's Paris banking career ended during the French Revolution, when he was suspected of saving many of his countrymen during a massacre of the Swiss by French troops. In the US, locals assumed him to be French and thus the community that grew up around his home became known as Frenchtown.

The Worman Grist Mill on Trenton Avenue is the oldest industrial structure in Frenchtown.

Within several years of Prevost's arrival, a blacksmith, two general stores, a sawmill and tavern comprised the town's commercial center. By the mid-1800s, a covered bridge connected Frenchtown to Uhlerstown, Pennsylvania; resident housing grew to more than two dozen homes and a branch of the Pennsylvania Railroad came to town.

But like many of its river-town counterparts, Frenchtown felt the migration of industry and commerce to more urban areas, and fell into an economic slump. Artists visited periodically throughout the years, but it has only been recently that they have invaded Frenchtown, transforming store fronts on Bridge and Race streets (the town's two main streets) into antiques shops, galleries with fine arts and crafts, and a proliferation of restaurants and cafés.

Even so, Frenchtown remains somewhat of a secret – a town still on the cusp of being discovered. "We're still pretty much a weekend town," one shopkeeper told me.

★ FAMOUS FACES

Writer **Nathaniel West** completed *Miss Lonelyhearts* in a rented room in Frenchtown. And in 1930, artist **Kurt Wiese**, best known for his illustrations for the original *Bambi* book, moved to Frenchtown and stayed until his death in 1974.

Sunup to Sundown

Hiking & Biking

When the old Pennsylvania Railroad tracks were removed in the 1980s, the railbed was turned into a path for bicyclists and pedestrians. A beautiful biking and walking stretch goes from Prallsville Mills in Stockton to Bull's Island Recreation Area and onward to Frenchtown.

Freeman's Bicycle Shop on Bridge Street in Frenchtown rents bikes; ☎ 908-996-7712.

★ TIP

New Jersey law requires that helmets be worn while bicycling.

Green Sergeant's Bridge

This beautiful wooden-covered ocher bridge in Sergeantsville is the last of the 75 covered bridges that once stood in New Jersey. You can drive through with your car but it's more fun to walk or bike. Rosemont-Ringoes Road (Route 604), between Rosemont and Sergeantsville.

Prallsville Mills

Prallsville Mills is listed on the National Register of Historic Places.

The **Delaware River Mill Society** preserves this former mill site, which consists of the main mill, the granary, the small linseed oil mill and the sawmill (the red frame building). The main mill is open to the public, and guides explain how the grist mill worked. Artsbridge, a collective of local painters, sculptors, crafters and writers, operates a gallery in the linseed building. Shows featuring antiques, art and sculpture, as well as concerts, are held throughout the year. Open Sundays from Memorial Day through August, 1 to 4 p.m. Route 29, Stockton; ☎ 609-397-3586.

Bull's Island Recreation Area

Located just north of Stockton, Bull's Island Recreation Area is the only section of the Delaware & Raritan Canal State Park where camping is permitted. There are 69 campsites on the island, complete with toilet and shower facilities, drinking water, fire rings and picnic tables (but no electric or water hookups). A pedestrian bridge connects the recreation area to Lumberville, Pennsylvania, and a launch ramp provides boat access to the Delaware River. Canoes and rowboats may be used in both the river and canal; powerboats are permitted only in the river. The camping season is from April 1 to October 31; $10 per night, per campsite.

2185 Daniel Bray Highway (Route 29), Stockton; ☎ 609-397-2949.

TUBING THE DELAWARE

From May to September, you can buy an inner tube at the Citgo gas station in Frenchtown for $10 and tube the Delaware. The experience is completely "self-serve," as you have to fill the tube with air and walk it to the river yourself. If you have transport back, you can tube all the way to New Hope/Lambertville.

★ TIP

New Jersey's Fish, Game & Wildlife Division stocks the canal with trout just below the lock at the entrance to Bull's Island Recreation Area.

Arts & Crafts

SUNFLOWER GLASS STUDIO

Karen and Geoff Caldwell have been creating their beautiful glass objects for more than 20 years. Karen is the designer, and Geoff, a master craftsman, produces the exotic glassware, ranging from home accessories such as candleholders, vases, picture frames and boxes, to windows and miniature glass houses. The studio is located midway between Stockton and Sergeantsville on Route 523 (877 Sergeantsville Road), ☎ 609-397-1535.

Sunflower Glass Studio made the stained-glass windows in one of the Woolverton Inn's cottages (see page 148).

RIVERBANK ARTS

Owned by print artist Susan Roseman and Peter Erricco, Riverbank Arts features the works of more than 100 area artists. Chock-full of etchings, paintings and drawings, the gallery is great for browsing. Open Monday, Tuesday and Wednesday, noon to 5 p.m.; Thursday and Sunday, 10 a.m. to 6 p.m.; and Friday and Saturday, 11 a.m. to 7 p.m. 19 Bridge Street, Stockton; ☎ 609-397-9330.

CANE FARM FURNITURE

One of America's oldest crafts is still practiced at this former chicken farm, where owner Phil Cane turned chicken coops into one of the country's largest furniture showrooms. Handmade re-creations of 17th- and 18th-century Early American, Colonial and Shaker furniture are featured. Open Friday and Saturday, 10 a.m. to 5 p.m.; Sunday, 1 to 5 p.m. Route 519, Rosemont; ☎ 609-397-0606.

DECOYS & WILDLIFE GALLERY

The largest decoy shop in the US is in Frenchtown. Ron Kobli moved his world-famous Decoys & Wildlife Gallery here more than a decade ago. Kobli specializes in hunting decoys (old and new), and the gallery features hundreds of them. Woodcarvings jump from every corner of the floor-to-ceiling racks; and gallery walls are lined with original paintings (most of wildlife) by top artists. 55 Bridge Street, Frenchtown; ☎ 908-996-6501.

BEYOND THE LOOKING GLASS GALLERY

An absolute Frenchtown must is Charles Klabunde's Beyond The Looking Glass Gallery. A master printmaker working in a disappearing art form – hand-etched copper engraving – Klabunde has been compared with such masters as Bosch, Dürer and Blake. He came to Frenchtown in 1999, after more than 30 years in New York City. Visitors can now watch him work, as well as view his seemingly endless display of etchings. 33 Bridge Street, Frenchtown; ☎ 908-996-6464.

☞ DID YOU KNOW?

Etchings by master printmaker Charles Klabunde of Frenchtown are part of permanent collections at The Metropolitan Museum of Art in New York, the National Gallery in Washington DC and the Philadelphia Art Museum.

Shop Till You Drop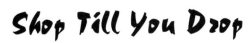

Stockton

PHILLIPS FINE WINES

This is no ordinary wine shop. Considered by many to be the top wine store in New Jersey, Phillips Fine Wines is almost a wine museum. Run by Richard Phillips, the charming store has several rooms with floor-to-ceiling racks of wines from around the world, including the best of California, Australia, France, Italy and Chile. The staff is knowledgeable and makes great recommendations. Open daily, Monday to Thursday, 9 a.m. to 9 p.m.; Friday and Saturday, 9 a.m. to 10 p.m.; Sunday, noon to 6 p.m. 17 Bridge Street, Stockton; ☎ 609-397-0587.

Frenchtown

B FRENCHTOWN

This famed Frenchtown boutique began years ago when Bucks County native Jennifer Barclay started block-printing her designs onto T-shirts at age 17 in her parents' garage. At the 1985 Lambertville Shad Festival, she introduced her wares to the public; soon after that she opened her first shop, then called Blue Fish, in Frenchtown. With the opening came success in the fashion world. Barclay's exclusive line is sold only at **B Frenchtown**, and every piece of her clothing is still hand-painted and signed. Open Thursday to Saturday, 10 a.m. to 6 p.m.; Sunday, noon to 5 p.m. 62 Trenton Avenue #1, Frenchtown, NJ; ☎ 908-996-3720.

★ FAMOUS FACES

When actor **Bill Cosby** wore a Blue Fish sweater on one of his TV shows, Frenchtown's clothing boutique went national.

THE STUDIO

This eclectic store is run by two former New Yorkers, one of whom oversaw the installation of The Cellar at Macy's Herald Square. Once a private mansion, the building has since housed a department store, the Gem Theater, and a bed & breakfast. Since the 1980s, the gothic Victorian structure has been home to The Studio, a haven of fine glass, garden accessories, florals, topiaries, soaps, furniture, fine linens and treasures. A gourmet food section was recently added, and delicacies can be shipped anywhere. Look for resident cats, Oona and Charlie. The Studio is open Wednesday through Friday, 10 a.m. to 5 p.m.; Saturday and Sunday, 10 a.m. to 6 p.m.; open seven days in December. 12 Bridge Street, Frenchtown; ☎ 908-996-7424.

NATURAL INSTINCTS
The owner of this nature-themed store is an avid bird-lover, and he's made it easy for others to share this interest. Everything a birdwatcher may want or need is here: Bushnell binoculars, feeders, nest boxes and unique garden wares. 23 Race Street, Frenchtown; ☎ 908-996-6304.

GARBO & SASHA
I liked this store before I ever entered it, simply because of its name. Unusual, eccentric items include great clothing, handcrafted jewelry and handsome furniture. 16 Race Street, Frenchtown; ☎ 908-996-7976.

BOOK GARDEN
The 19th-century Victorian housing this independent bookstore creates the perfect ambience for the wonderful books sold here. An entire room is devoted to used books. 28 Bridge Street, Frenchtown; ☎ 908-996-2022.

TANTE KRINGLE CHRISTMAS COTTAGE
This festive shop, open March through December, features hand-blown glass from Europe and hand-carved ornaments from Germany. The store is typically open Thursday through Sunday; call for hours. 106 Harrison, Frenchtown; ☎ 908-996-2750.

Best Places to Stay

ACCOMMODATIONS PRICE SCALE

*Price scale is based on a standard room
for two persons, per night.*

Inexpensive . . . . under $100
Moderate . . . . $100-$200
Expensive . . . . $201-$300
Deluxe . . . . more than $300

THE WOOLVERTON INN
6 Woolverton Road
Stockton, NJ
☎ 888-AN-INN-4-U or 609-397-0802
Expensive to Deluxe

An excerpt from the guestbook at The Woolverton Inn reads, "There's a small hotel that doesn't need a wishing well... Richard Rodgers, you stayed at the wrong hotel. – 4/20/01, Bill and Trudy."

While several inns offer accommodations along this side of the river, *the* place to stay is The Woolverton. Three friends from Chicago purchased this 1792 stone manor house in 1999 and have transformed it into a luxurious yet unpretentious country estate.

"We looked at inns from New Hampshire to North Carolina, and finally settled in an area we really love – that's rich in history and natural beauty," says co-owner Matthew Lovette. "We traded honking cars for honking geese and steel for fieldstone. We absolutely love our new life and haven't looked back."

The threesome's love for their new life is contagious. From the moment you turn onto the oak-lined drive (just minutes from "downtown" Stockton), the sense of civilized country living is apparent. Resident sheep Betty and Pâté graze contentedly among wild-flowers in the meadows. A wooden swing dangles invitingly from a magnolia tree. Upper and lower porches run the length of the inn and, inside the historic house, floors are wide-planked, the custom-made furnishings are tasteful and comfortable, and Matthew's oatmeal-raisin cookies are outrageously good.

Breakfast (served by candlelight in winter, or outside in summer) is even more decadent. House specialties include homemade apple-cranberry turkey sausage, lemon-ricotta pancakes, apple streusel en papillote, orange-cranberry scones, vegetable frittata with caramelized onions and Costa Rican coffee.

Fresh-cut flowers, fluffy robes, fireplaces, feather beds, in-room massages and spa-like baths are just a few of the amenities that await guests in both the main house (with eight rooms and suites) and five private cottages. Be forewarned: once you check in, you will never want to leave.

The luxury cottages are spectacular, with sweeping views of the adjacent woodlands and protected farmland. My personal favorite is the two-level Sojourn Loft, which has an exotic travel theme. The first floor features a tiered fireplace faced in Venetian plaster with Persian-derived motifs; on the second level there is another fireplace, and a huge, oversized hammock for two in the spa bath.

The Cotswold Cottage, next to the sheep pasture, takes on an English theme. A sliding barn door reveals a whirlpool tub and a mural depicting the English countryside by contemporary New Hope artist John Schmitburger. The Hunterdon Cottage features a 20-foot cupola topping a retractable canopy over the bed. The Audubon Cottage, nature-themed, offers the grandest views of the estate.

> ### ✖ HISTORIC TRIVIA
>
> John Prall, Jr., who built The Woolverton Inn as his home in 1792, was once crossing the Delaware River in a small boat when the boat suddenly capsized. As the raging waters rushed by him, he clung to a large rock that kept him safe until he could be rescued. Prall went back to the river soon after and had the rock removed and embedded into of the stone walls of the home for good luck.

The Woolverton was originally built as a private home by John Prall, the wealthy pioneer merchant and Revolutionary War officer who owned and operated the Prallsville Mill just down the hill. The home remained in the Prall family until the mid-1800s, when Maurice Woolverton purchased the estate. Woolverton made sweeping changes to the manor house, giving it an eclectic style combining 18th- and 19th-century elements. His additions included the inn's front porch, a second-floor balcony, fan windows over the doors, and a mansard roof with intricate ironwork. The house later became the home of Singent Terell – founder of the world-renowned (but now defunct) Lambertville Music Circus, and originator of the Washington Crossing the Delaware re-enactment each year on Christmas Day. Many famous radio and theater personalities frequently stayed at the Terell house.

⭐ **FAMOUS FACES**

Ella Fitzgerald and **The Supremes** are among the notables who performed at the Lambertville Music Circus and stayed at the Woolverton house during the time it was owned by Singent Terell.

THE STOCKTON INN
1 Main Street
Stockton
☎ 609-397-1250
Inexpensive to Moderate

Lodging caught on at this historic inn in 1935, when reporters, covering the Hauptmann-Lindbergh kidnapping trial in nearby Flemington, needed a place to sleep. The inn was renovated in the 1980s and reopened with 11 rooms and suites, all featuring private baths, canopy beds and fireplaces. One room and two suites are located in the main house above the restaurant (see page 154), and the remainder of the accommodations are scattered throughout adjacent carriage houses and a home directly across the street from the inn.

SILVER MAPLE ORGANIC FARM AND BED & BREAKFAST
Route 523, PO Box 156
Sergeantsville
☎ 908-237-2192, www.silvermaplefarm.com
Moderate

This three-room inn, housed in a 200-year-old farmhouse, opened in November of 2000. Rooms are tastefully decorated, with lots of sun-splashed color on moldings and in fabrics to add interest. But the real draw is the farm. Immediately after purchasing the inn, owners Steve Noll (a former florist) and Bill Hawley (once an editor) planted several acres of vegetables, flowers and herbs. The farm is completely organic and the harvested goods are sold to local restaurants. Goats, with names like Lucy and Ricky (brother and sister) and Thelma and Louise (sisters), are another highlight, as are the owners' two Pembroke Welsh corgis, who have the run of the farm. A full country breakfast is served, and there's a roaring fireplace, swimming pool and outdoor hot tub. Children and pets are welcome by arrangement.

THE GUESTHOUSE AT FRENCHTOWN
85 Ridge Road
Frenchtown
☎ 908-996-7474
www.frenchtownguesthouse.com
Moderate

If you've always wanted to live in the country, or at least try it for a time, the Guesthouse at Frenchtown is perfect. When you rent this 1780 Colonial fieldstone home, it's all yours – living room with fireplace and wide-plank wood floors; dining room with another open-hearth fireplace; full kitchen with modern-day amenities; and two bedrooms, each with bath. The house accommodates two couples traveling together, or one couple with children (over 12). And you don't necessarily have to cook; several Frenchtown restaurants will cater meals, and one chef will even come to the house to prepare it. However, breakfast (yogurt, cereals, bagels, coffee, juice and fruit) is included. Weekly rates are available.

Daytime visits from family and friends (up to 12 invitees) are welcome.

WIDOW McCREA HOUSE
53 Kingwood Avenue
Frenchtown
☎ 908-996-4999, www.widowmccrea.com
Inexpensive to Moderate

The widow Frances McCrea commissioned this Italianate Victorian house in 1878. For many years, the house has served as a quiet bed & breakfast, featuring four elegant rooms, queen-size feather beds, antiques and gourmet candlelight breakfasts. In November of 2001, a separate private cottage with an antique brass Victorian featherbed, fireplace, comfy sofa and Jacuzzi, was added (along with an antique table for private in-room candlelight breakfasts). Guests can walk to Frenchtown shops or borrow bikes from the innkeeper.

Best Places to Eat

DINING PRICE SCALE
Pricing includes one entrée, with glass of wine and coffee.
Inexpensive . . . . under $20
Moderate . . . . $20-$35
Expensive . . . . over $35

American

STOCKTON INN
1 Main Street
Stockton
☎ 609-397-1250
Moderate to Expensive

The murals on the dining room walls of the Stockton Inn were painted during the depression by local artists, who traded their work for food and drink.

This ancient inn, constructed of local stone, was built in 1710 as a private residence. The site of the residence was chosen on the advice of the Lenni Lenape Indians who warned of flooding in the valley. Despite some high floods over the years, the Stockton Inn has always been spared.

The mansion was transformed into a restaurant and inn in the 1830s and has remained so ever since. Under the ownership of the Colligan family from 1922 to 1983, the inn housed an eclectic set of pets – from Saint Bernards to deer – and attracted an entourage of artists.

In 1933, Lorenz Hart and Richard Rodgers were so inspired by the inn and its stone wishing well that they wrote the song *There's a Small Hotel*, which debuted in their 1936 Broadway hit *On Your Toes*.

During the famed Lindbergh-Hauptmann trial years in nearby Flemington, the inn became a favorite hangout for reporters in need of a place to eat and sleep. In the 1940s, bandleader Paul Whiteman kept a regular table at the inn, and signed off his radio and TV shows announcing he was "going to dinner at Ma Colligan's."

Now under the caring hand of chef Robert Koenig, the Stockton Inn has maintained its reputation for fine dining. Warm brie with port wine blackberry sauce is a nice starter for entrées such as almond-crusted rack of lamb, roast Long Island duckling or, for the vegetarians among us, portobello mushroom ravioli with arugula, sun-dried tomatoes and kalamata olives in roasted garlic. Dining rooms feature murals and fireplaces; in nice weather, alfresco dining overlooking the inn's waterfalls and pond is popular.

★ FAMOUS FACES

During the 1940s, a table at the Stockton Inn, which was favored by **F. Scott Fitzgerald**, **Damon Runyon**, **Dorothy Parker**, **S.J. Perelman**, and **Robert Benchley**, became known as the Algonquin Round Table in honor of the writers' New York City hangout.

MEIL'S
Bridge and Main Streets
Stockton
☎ 609-397-8033
BYOB; no credit cards
Moderate to Expensive

This tiny café across the street from The Stockton Inn offers a blend of sophisticated yet down-home comfort food. Meil's is as famous for its meatloaf as for its pesto rotini with goat cheese, and you can order Thanksgiving dinner (with all of the trimmings) year-round. The atmosphere is casual, cozy and 1940s funky. Open seven days for breakfast, lunch and dinner.

SERGEANTSVILLE INN
601 Rosemont-Ringoes Road
Sergeantsville
☎ 609-397-3700
Moderate to Expensive

This 1700s stone inn is a good reason to visit Sergeantsville. Once a private residence, the building has served as a grocery store, an ice cream parlor, a feed store, and a pelt-trading post before being converted to a restaurant in the mid-1980s. Game is the specialty here – ostrich, antelope, kangaroo, buffalo, venison and wild boar – as are the martinis. Thirty-four different martinis are listed on the menu, with such names as Lady Godiva (Stoli Kafya with Godiva liqueur, Kahlua and espresso); Creamsicle (Stoli Ohranj, Stoli Vanil, Licor 43 and a splash of orange juice); and Old Blue Eyes (Bombay Sapphire gin with dry vermouth and Blue Curaçao). The wine list is also extensive, featuring multinational choices from Lebanon and South Africa.

Dinner begins with bread and olive oil flavored with oregano, thyme, rosemary and fresh-ground pepper, and is followed by soup or salad (included with dinner). Aside from game, all of the American favorites are offered, including duck, lamb, pork tenderloin, filet mignon, fish and some vegetarian and pasta dishes.

★ CULINARY SECRET

Erricco's Market in Stockton (☎ 609-397-0049) was once an old train station. It's been converted into a small gourmet deli and is a great place to pick up a snack for a picnic or stroll along the Delaware River.

Continental

ATRIO CAFE
515 Bridge Street
Stockton
☎ 609-397-0042
BYOB
Moderate to Expensive

Locals love this casual but elegant restaurant, so be sure to make a reservation. The menu changes continuously, as the chef knows his herbs and spices and successfully experiments with farm-fresh produce and ingredients. Salads are wonderful, as are the lamb chops and the grilled fish. Crab cakes are the house specialty. Atrio Café is open for dinner only, Tuesday through Sunday.

★ CULINARY SECRET

For great bagels and homemade pastries, try the **Bridge Café**, just steps from the Delaware River in Frenchtown. 8 Bridge Street; ☎ 908-996-6040.

FRENCHTOWN INN
7 Bridge Street
Frenchtown
☎ 908-996-3300
Expensive

Even before Frenchtown was "discovered," locals knew of The Frenchtown Inn. The inn, known as the Lower Hotel, prospered in the Roaring Twenties, then gradually slid into disrepair during the Depression, which caused the decline of river and rail traffic. Writer **Nathaniel West** boarded here during the 1930s and wrote most of his works while in residence.

In 1985, the dilapidated boarding house/tavern was transformed into three dining rooms and a bar area, and quickly gained a reputation for fine dining. Current owner and chef Andrew Tomko purchased the inn in 1996. He is well known for his signature sesame seed-crusted salmon, roast game hen on capellini vegetables, and brie in puff pastry with white grape cream sauce.

International

ROSEMONT CAFE
Corner of 519 and 604
Rosemont
☎ 609-397-4097
BYOB
Moderate

Housed in an old general store, this roadside café, complete with wide-plank hardwood floors, is reminiscent of the Whistle Stop Café in the movie *Fried Green Tomatoes*, except this version is more elegant and artsy. "Eat Globally, Drive Locally" is the theme of Wednesday night dinners, which feature a three-course menu from a different section of the globe (Africa, Mexico, Scandinavia and Lebanon are among the regions that have been represented). We tried Greek night, which offered green lentil soup with sorrel and tomato, a choice of cinnamon lamb casserole or eggplant with spiced tomato sauce, and home-baked baklava for dessert. The regular menu is enticing, too. Lunch is brunch-like, with selections such as omelets, French toast, or baked burrito sandwiches, while dinner ranges from pastas (shrimp and braised fennel in saffron cream sauce) to fish (haddock with roasted pepper, shallot and olive confit). Desserts are made on the premises, probably from one of the hundreds of cookbooks lining the old general store shelves.

The café features artwork provided by Riverbank Arts, which represents over 100 area artists. Displays are changed every three to four weeks, and all selections are for sale.

Open for breakfast on weekdays from 8 a.m., weekends from 9 a.m. Dinner is served Wednesday through Sunday, from 6 p.m.; closed Mondays.

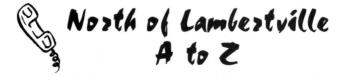

North of Lambertville A to Z

Animal Hospital

Lambertville Animal Clinic, 66 York Street, Lambertville, NJ, ☎ 609-397-3657.

Banks

Hudson United Bank, 21 Bridge Street, Frenchtown, NJ, ☎ 908-996-2918.

Food Markets

Sergeantsville General Store, 600 Rosemont-Ringoes Road, Sergeantsville, NJ, ☎ 609-397-3214.

A&P Food Stores, 28 6th Street, Frenchtown, NJ, ☎ 908-996-6869.

Frenchtown Country Market, 1 Lott Street, Frenchtown, NJ, ☎ 908-996-6100.

Gas Stations

Exxon Heath's Service, 83 Bridge Street, Lambertville, NJ, ☎ 609-397-0433.

Cifelli's Sunoco, Inc., 82 Bridge Street, Lambertville, NJ, ☎ 609-397-1212.

Citgo Service Center, 11 Frenchtown Road, Frenchtown, NJ, ☎ 908-996-4223.

Hospital

Hunterdon Medical Center, 2100 Westcott Drive, Flemington, NJ, ☎ 908-788-6100.

Movie Theater

Cinema Plaza, 240 US Highway 202 & 31, Flemington, NJ, ☎ 908-782-2777.

Newspapers

Hunterdon County Democrat, 18 Minneakoning Road, Flemington, NJ, ☎ 908-782-4747.

Delaware Valley News, 207 Harrison Street, Frenchtown, NJ, ☎ 908-996-4047.

Pharmacies

Frenchtown Pharmacy, 9 Kingwood Avenue, Frenchtown, NJ, ☎ 908-996-4180.

Post Offices

Stockton, 2 Bridge Street, ☎ 609-397-0940.

Rosemont, Cane Farm Furniture, ☎ 609-397-2761.

Religious Services

Amwell Church of the Brethren, 40 Sandbrook Headquarters Road, Stockton, NJ, ☎ 609-397-0514.

Brethren Church Sergeantsville, 522 Rosemont-Ringoes Road, Stockton, NJ, ☎ 609-397-9118.

Kingwood United Methodist, Route 519, Kingwood, ☎ 908-996-6803.

Sandy Ridge Community Church, 47 Sandy Ridge Road, Stockton, NJ, ☎ 609-397-0371.

Stockton Presbyterian Church, 22 South Main Street, Stockton, NJ, ☎ 609-397-0130.

Stockton Wesleyan Church, 12 North Main Street, Stockton, NJ, ☎ 609-397-7288.

Finesville United Methodist Church, 14 3rd Street, Frenchtown, NJ, ☎ 908-996-4439.

Frenchtown Baptist Church, 2nd Street, Frenchtown, NJ, ☎ 908-996-2370.

Frenchtown Presbyterian Church, 20 4th Street, Frenchtown, NJ, ☎ 908-996-2227.

Frenchtown United Methodist, 16 3rd Street, Frenchtown, NJ, ☎ 908-996-3117.

United Reformed Church, 99 Horseshoe Bend Road, Frenchtown, NJ, ☎ 908-996-4343.

Wine & Spirits

Phillips Fine Wines, 17 Bridge Street, Stockton, NJ, ☎ 609-397-0587.

Doylestown

Doylestown rivals many large cities such as nearby Philadelphia with its world-class cultural facilities, elegant Victorian architecture and historic attractions. Its commitment to the arts is exceeded only by its ingrained preservation ethic.

– National Trust for Historic Preservation, 2001

Absolutely no journey to the Delaware River Valley is complete without at least a day-trip to the area's cultural centers – Doylestown, Pennsylvania (just west of New Hope); and Princeton, New Jersey (east of Lambertville). The two centers are different in scope; Doylestown is known for its astounding collection of museums, Princeton for its world-famous university, architecture and upscale shopping.

History

The longtime Bucks County seat (since 1813), Doylestown takes its name from **Edward Doyle**, who settled here with his family after purchasing 150 acres of land from Pennsylvania's founder, **William Penn**. In 1745, Edward Doyle's son William was licensed to operate a tavern, and for the next 30-plus years the village was known as "William Doyle's Tavern." William sold the tavern in 1776, after which the town became known by its present name.

Doylestown's historic district includes nearly 1,200 buildings, and is listed on the National Register of Historic Places.

Sunup to Sundown

Doylestown's "Mercer Mile," home to Fonthill, the Moravian Pottery and Tile Works, and The Mercer Museum, showcases the accomplishments of one man – Henry Chapman Mercer.

Today, just an hour from downtown Philadelphia, Doylestown is a happy mix of Colonial, Federal and Victorian architecture, and upscale, hometown charm. "You can walk to everything – doctor, dentist, stores, school... " one resident proudly told me. But it's the town's four world-class museums for which Doylestown has become known; all are within walking distance of the town's residential areas.

Three of the museums – the **Fonthill**, the **Moravian Pottery & Tile Works**, and **The Mercer Museum** – are poured, reinforced concrete "castles," built by former Doylestown resident **Henry Chapman Mercer**, a noted anthropologist, archaeologist, historian, writer, innovator and collector.

The Arts

Doylestown's Museums

FONTHILL

Fonthill has 18 fireplaces, 32 stairwells, more than 200 windows, and over 900 prints and other objects that Mercer gathered from throughout the world.

Henry Chapman Mercer began work on Fonthill, his private home, at age 52. He described the home as "an interweaving of my own fancies blending with memories of my travels and suggestions from engravings."

Fonthill stands on 60 acres of rolling lawns and woods at the end of an avenue of sycamores. The interior can be seen only by guided tour, and the 44-room mansion is definitely worth seeing.

Doylestown

N

.5 MILE

.8 KM

© 2002 HUNTER PUBLISHING, INC.

1. Fordhook Farm
2. Our Lady of Czestochowa; Pearl S. Buck House (Green Hill Farm)
3. Malmark Bellcraftsmen
4. Moravian Pottery & Tile Works
5. Highland Farms
6. Fonthill Museum
7. County Theater
8. James A. Michener Museum
9. The Mercer Museum
10. Barley Sheaf Farm

Mercer traveled extensively, and his passion for the arts was encouraged by his very wealthy Aunt Elizabeth, a sort of "Auntie Mame" character who took him to see Rhineland castles. When Aunt Elizabeth died in 1905, she left Mercer her considerable fortune. Although Mercer lived in Fonthill, the house was planned to serve as a museum to display his collections, primarily tiles, including ancient Babylonian clay tablets, delft, Chinese roof tiles, and his own spectacular decorative tile works. Almost every interior surface is encrusted with hundreds of multi-colored clay tiles, many of which tell stories: biblical tales, the exploration of the New World and Blue-beard's castle, to name a few.

✕ HISTORIC TRIVIA

In 1912, in celebration of the com-pletion of Fonthill, Mercer climbed onto the roof of his mansion, doused a large pyre of scrap lum-ber with kerosene and set it ablaze (the dreamlike medieval home was constructed entirely of fireproof concrete). Nearby, a poor washer-woman saw the conflagration and rushed, terrified, to the bedside of her adopted son, a five-year-old orphan. The orphan was future multimillionaire-author James A. Michener; the fire was his earliest memory.

Doylestown's famed "Mercer Tiles" have been used in the Gardner Museum in Boston, the Pennsylvania state capitol in Harrisburg and the National Press Club in Washington DC.

Fonthill is operated by the Bucks County Historical Society and is open daily for guided tours; reserva-tions are necessary. Monday to Saturday, 10 a.m. to 5 p.m.; Sunday, noon to 5 p.m. 225 East Court Street, ☎ 215-348-9461.

MORAVIAN POTTERY & TILE WORKS
Adjacent to Fonthill is the Moravian Pottery & Tile Works, which produced tiles and mosaics for floors, walls and ceilings. This Spanish-mission-style buil-ding replaced Henry Mercer's original tile studio, In-

dian House, which burned around the time Fonthill was completed. The Moravian Pottery & Tile Works was a successful business, flourishing during the heyday of the Arts and Crafts Movement. Mercer tiles were shipped worldwide, and were used in many notable buildings.

The Bucks County Department of Parks and Recreation now operates the tile works as a living museum. Visitors can view a video explaining the history of the works and then take a self-guided tour. Mercer's designs, glazes and processes are still used, and the tile works' artisans are happy to answer questions. The museum is open daily, with self-guided tours every half-hour. 130 Swamp Road (a short stroll from Fonthill), ☎ 215-345-6722.

THE MERCER MUSEUM
Tiles were only one facet of Henry Mercer's eclectic collection. He also adored traditional American tools that were made obsolete by 19th-century industrialization. When the tile works was finished in 1912, Mercer set his crew (which included his horse, Lucy, who actually received a paycheck) working on a museum to house his tool collection. The museum, Mercer's final castle, is a towering concrete confection of gables, windows and stairways. A central court is surrounded by seven stories of glassed-in galleries, each of which displays the tools of a different trade or craft.

More than 40,000 tools and utensils are featured in the museum and, quite frankly, you have to see it to believe it. Among the notable articles are a horse-drawn hearse and wicker coffin, a whaling boat, prison gallows, and baby carriages hanging from the

Henry Chapman Mercer's uncle lost a priceless armor collection in a catastrophic fire. That event is what inspired Mercer to build his own home out of concrete.

ceiling. Open daily. 84 South Pine Street, ☎ 215-345-0210.

JAMES A. MICHENER ART MUSEUM

Michener brought us the idea (of the museum). He probably envisioned a roomful of busts with spotlights on them. But as we began working on it, we thought, if you're going to create a monument to creativity, the monument had better be creative.

— Brian Peterson, Chief Curator

Built on the site of the old Bucks County prison (demolished in 1985), the James A. Michener Art Museum is a living tribute to the famous author, as well as to other prominent Bucks County artists, such as writers S.J. Perelman, Moss Hart, Pearl S. Buck, Dorothy Parker, Oscar Hammerstein II, and George S. Kaufman; painters Edward Hicks, Edward Redfield, Daniel Garber and Charles Sheeler; and archeologist, collector and tile maker Henry Chapman Mercer.

✖ HISTORIC TRIVIA

Author James Michener lived in eight Doylestown houses as a boy.

An entire room is devoted to Michener, where you'll find a replica of the office where he wrote his famous works, including *Hawaii, Chesapeake, Poland,* and the 1948 Pulitzer Prize-winning *Tales of the South Pacific,* along with his typewriter, chair, desk, dictionary and gypsy witch fortune-telling cards.

SOUTH PACIFIC

James Michener's writing career ignited when the author was 40 years old. Another Doylestown resident, **Oscar Hammerstein**, turned Michener's book *Tales of the South Pacific* into the hit musical *South Pacific*. Michener reportedly refused to bow to studio directors, who wanted to remove interracial themes from the story. All of Michener's works touched on religious and racial tolerance, hard work and self-reliance – themes that made him popular with the masses.

The Michener Museum also salutes Bucks County's 18th-century Impressionist painters, the New Hope modernists, and woodworker George Nakashima. Paintings included in the Impressionist collection include Edward Redfield's *The Burning of Centre Bridge* (1923) and a mural by Daniel Garber.

LOST AND FOUND

A 22-foot mural by **Daniel Garber**, titled "A Wooded Watershed," was donated to the Mont Alto (Pennsylvania) branch of Penn State University shortly after Garber painted it in 1926. The mural served as a backdrop for the school's auditorium, but was eventually packed away, and was lost and forgotten for 60 years. In 1992, a campus archiver contacted the Michener Museum and a state grant helped to return the mural to its rightful place in Bucks County.

Doylestown

Another collection at the Michener Museum, called **Creative Bucks County**, pays tribute to some of the artists and celebrities who've made their homes here. In a living room-like setting devoted to Kaufman and Hart, Hart's guestbook is opened to a page signed by an irate Alexander Woollcott, which reads, "This is to certify that, on my first visit to Moss Hart's house, I had one of the most unpleasant evenings I can recall ever having spent." Hart remarked to Kaufman that at least Woollcott hadn't broken his leg and been forced to stay on for weeks; this remark was the genesis for Kaufman's classic play, *The Man Who Came to Dinner*.

A tribute to Pearl S. Buck, who lived on a nearby 400-acre farm after writing *The Good Earth*, features a wall full of color snapshots of children – representing the more than 25,000 mixed-race children in the Far East who have been helped through the Pearl S. Buck foundation.

Just across the way, visitors can pick up the receiver of a 1930s telephone and hear Dorothy Parker sounding fierce, or put on headsets and listen to Paul Robeson singing Hammerstein's lyrics to *Old Man River*, or step up to a mock newsstand and read one of S.J. Perelman's short, savage comic turns from *The New Yorker*. A screening room runs film clips from movies featuring works of Bucks County artists.

The latest addition to the museum is the **Patricia A. Pfundt Sculpture Garden**, featuring sculpture placed among fountains, pathways and trees, as well as a special exhibit based on a cell from the old jail.

The Michener museum is open Tuesday through Friday, 10 a.m. to 4:30 p.m.; Wednesday, until 9 p.m.; Saturday and Sunday, 10 a.m. to 5 p.m.; closed Mondays. Admission is $6 for adults; children 12 and under are admitted free. 138 South Pine Street, ☎ 215-340-9800, www.michenerartmuseum.org.

Doylestown's Cultural Heritage

Aside from museums, Doylestown offers an array of must-sees. The following are among the more notable.

THE BEN SOLOWEY STUDIO

From 1929 to 1942, Ben Solowey led a dual life as both a celebrated easel painter and as one of the court artists to the Broadway kingdom. At the height of his acclaim, Solowey left the comforts of Fifth Avenue for the countryside of Bucks County. In 1936, he purchased a 34-acre farm with a dilapidated colonial farmhouse and barn and, in 1942, he and his wife, Rae, moved permanently to Bucks County. Solowey restored the circa-1765 farmhouse, rebuilt the property's summer kitchen as a guest house and transformed the barn into a spacious studio – which today, filled with his artwork, stands as a testament to his phenomenal talent.

Commissioned by *The New York Times* and the *New York Herald Tribune*, Solowey defined an era with his striking charcoal portraits of luminaries of the performing arts. Unlike many artists in the field, he insisted on working from life, and often visited the theater during rehearsals to delineate the performer either right on stage (frequently under a bare light bulb) or in a dressing room. To be drawn by

Solowey was a sign that the performer had "made it."

★ FAMOUS FACES

Actress **Ethel Barrymore** gave Ben Solowey an hour and 10 minutes to paint her – as much time as she'd ever given to anybody. Barrymore was so enchanted with the portrait that she autographed the work in the upper right-hand corner. On April 7, 1929, the drawing appeared in *The New York Times*, and Ben Solowey's second career was launched. He went on to draw nearly 900 portraits over the next 13 years – all from life.

After Ben's death in 1978, Rae insisted that his studio remain intact for the public to enjoy. The studio mounts at least two interpretative exhibitions of Ben's work per year, along with shows of present-day painters working in a similar vein. Nothing in the studio is roped or under glass, conveying the uncanny felling that Ben Solowey has just stepped away from his easel and will be back at any minute. 3551 Olde Bedminster Road, Bedminster, PA, (a short distance north of Doylestown). Call for exhibits and hours. ☎ 215-795-0228, www.solowey.com.

CINEMA

Movies made their debut in Doylestown in 1907 when **Hellyer's Movie House** opened on South Main Street; two years later, Hellyer's moved across the street to **Lenape Hall**, where it operated until 1925. In that year the **Strand Theatre**, Doylestown's first "real" movie theater was built. In 1938, the Strand was replaced by the new **County Theater**, which has remained – with nostalgic flair.

BUCKS COUNTY MOVIE TRIVIA

Movies featuring the work of Bucks County artists include these classics.

- *Oklahoma!*
- *Casablanca*
- *Lassie Come Home*
- *Meet Me in St. Louis*
- *Hawaii*
- *West Side Story*
- *Kiss Me Kate*
- *The Man Who Came to Dinner*
- *Show Boat*
- *The King and I*
- *A Star is Born* (1937)

The '40s, '50s and '60s were golden years for the theater but, by the 1970s, TV, shopping centers and multiplexes took their toll, sending the theater into a slow, downward spiral. In the early '80s, the neon letters on the marquee tower went dim one by one. It wasn't until 1992, when the theater was leased by **Closely Watched Films**, a local film society that had been showing art films in Doylestown, that the art deco-style theater was saved from extinction.

Closely Watched cleaned, painted and renovated the theater and today is its proud owner.

Stop by during the week for artsy, foreign films or on Sundays for viewings of black-and-white classics like the original *A Street Car Named Desire*, with Vivian Leigh and Marlon Brando, or *Sabrina,* starring Audrey Hepburn. Discussions sometimes follow. Saturday afternoons are devoted to kids' matinees, with unusual offerings like *Betty Boop*, *The Phantom Tollbooth* and *Bugs Bunny*. County Theater, 20 East State Street, ☎ 215-345-6789.

★ FAMOUS FACES

Dorothy Parker and her second husband, Alan Campbell, bought a 14-room country house (Fox House) on 111 acres near Doylestown. The property had an apple orchard, barn, and view of the Delaware River and, at $4,500, was a steal. Dorothy did little writing at Fox House but reportedly attended movies often at County Theater.

Huge, colorful panels of stained glass inside Doylestown's National Shrine of Our Lady of Czestochowa depict the history of Christianity in Poland and the US.

Historic Sites

Our Lady of Czestochowa

The story of this massive shrine and church began in 1953 when Father Michael M. Zembrzuski, a Pauline monk from Poland, purchased a small parcel of farmland near Doylestown. Two years later, he converted a small barn into a chapel and solemnly dedicated it to Our Lady of Czestochowa. With the approach of Poland's millennium came a wish to build a large shrine. In October of 1966, Archbishop John Krol and President Lyndon B. Johnson greeted nearly 100,000 pilgrims who had journeyed to Doylestown for the historic dedication of the new shrine. Today, the property encompasses 170 acres, and is home to a large church, a monastery, a cemetery, a gift shop and a cafeteria. A Polish-American festival (see *Festivals & Events*) is held every fall. The complex is on Ferry Road, Doylestown; hours for the shrine are 7:15 a.m. to 4:30 p.m., daily. ☎ 215-345-0600.

Pearl S. Buck House

Author Pearl S. Buck moved to this 1835 farmhouse, **Green Hills Farm**, in 1934. She lived here for 38 years until her death, just days before her 81st birthday, and is buried on the 60-acre farm.

Now a National Historic Landmark, Buck's house, with a unique blend of Chinese and 19th-century Pennsylvania arts and architecture, is open for guided tours. Her many literary and humanitarian awards are on display, including the Nobel and Pulitzer prizes for literature for her book *The Good Earth*. Buck published more than 70 books, was active in the American civil rights and women's rights movements and founded the **Pearl S. Buck Foundation**, which provides sponsorship funding for thousands of children in Asian countries. 520 Dublin Road, Dublin, PA; ☎ 215-249-0100 or 800-220-BUCK, www.pearlsbuck.org.

Bell Makers

The world's largest manufacturer of fine-tuned English handbells began in Doylestown and now operates studios in nearby Plumsteadville. **Malmark, Inc., Bellcraftsmen**, opened its doors in Doylestown in 1974 after founder Jacob Malta developed a new design for a handbell, which included features he felt would benefit ringers and advance the art of ringing. The bells are bronze and are used throughout the world by handbell choirs. Individual tours of the facility are available by appointment, and interested visitors can place orders for bells. Malmark, Inc. is on Route 611 (Bell Crest Park), Plumsteadville; ☎ 215-766-7200 or 800-HANDBELL, www.malmark.com.

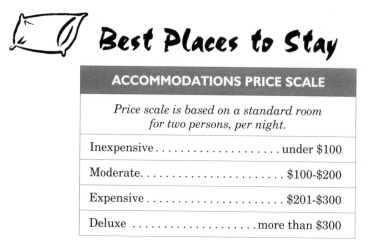

Best Places to Stay

ACCOMMODATIONS PRICE SCALE
Price scale is based on a standard room for two persons, per night.
Inexpensive . . . . under $100
Moderate. . . . . $100-$200
Expensive . . . . $201-$300
Deluxe . . . . more than $300

THE INN AT FORDHOOK FARM

105 New Britain Road
Doylestown
☎ 215-345-1766
Children 12 and over welcome
Expensive to Deluxe

This luxurious, 60-acre country estate was the long-time home of W. Atlee Burpee, founder of the Burpee Seed Company. Now a luxury inn (still owned by the Burpee Company), The Inn at Fordhook Farm features six upscale rooms with amenities such as 11-foot ceilings, floor-to-ceiling windows, French doors, original Mercer-tiled fireplaces, antique French beds and Persian rugs.

A highlight of a stay at Fordhook is, of course, the gardens. The 18th-century stone house is surrounded by 200-year-old linden trees. Fordhook Farm was the foundation of Burpee's plant breeding programs, and subsequently became the birthplace of countless innovations in American vegetable and flower breeding. Soon after purchasing the farm, Burpee began testing seeds and selling them – a revolution in the American seed industry, as the common practice at the time was to rely on European bulk suppliers. The grounds are still used for experimental gardens.

Doylestown

✕ HISTORIC TRIVIA

The Fordhook lima bean, Golden Bantam corn, iceberg lettuce and Big Boy tomatoes were some of the vegetable products developed at Fordhook Farm. Flowers include petunias, snapdragons, impatiens, white marigolds, and zinnias.

BARLEY SHEAF FARM
5281 York Road (Route 202)
Holicong
☎ 215-794-5104
www.barleysheaf.com
Moderate to Expensive

Pulitzer Prize-winning journalist and playwright George S. Kaufman and his wife, Beatrice, bought this Bucks County estate in 1936 and lived here for nearly two decades. Under their ownership, the farm served as a gathering place for some of Broadway's luminaries, among them Moss Hart, Dorothy Parker, and the Marx Brothers. Kaufman's croquet games at the farm were reportedly legendary.

It was Beatrice who found the property. Visiting a childhood friend in Bucks County, she heard that a country estate owned by the then-director of New York's Whitney Museum was up for sale. Beatrice phoned Kaufman in Manhattan to insist that he would love it – that no one was around, that there was no social life, only quiet country people who minded their own business. Kaufman reluctantly took the train from Penn Station to examine the farm himself and, won over, told his wife the place was hers if she wanted it. The purchase was big news in the local newspaper, *The Intelligencer* of Doylestown. On Sept. 24, 1936, reporter W. Lester Trauch wrote, "Bucks County's literary colony, which includes Pearl S. Buck and Dorothy Parker, will add to its brilliant list of newcomers, Mr. and Mrs. George S. Kaufman... "

Kaufman dubbed his new home Cherchez La Farm. Prior to the Kaufmans' purchase, the house had acquired at least three additions, giving it a rambling, almost whimsical look; they pumped an estimated $100,000 more into renovations on the old home, including a new kitchen – a theme he explored in his comedy *George Washington Slept Here*, which ran for 173 performances in New York before being filmed with Jack Benny as the star in 1942.

Set at the end of a long, tree-lined drive far back from the busy highway, the three-story fieldstone main house looks much as it did in Kaufman's day. Now owned by a family who relocated from Switzerland to run the farm as a bed-and-breakfast, Barley Sheaf offers gracious rooms and suites with private baths, Jacuzzis and working fireplaces. Barley Boy, the family's Bernese mountain dog, is a favorite among guests, as are the sheep who graze out back, wearing clanking Swiss bells around their necks. Barley Sheaf Farm is located on Route 202, midway between Doylestownand New Hope.

★ FAMOUS FACES

John Steinbeck and **George S. Kaufman** worked on *Of Mice and Men* while at Barley Sheaf Farm.

Doylestown

OSCAR HAMMERSTEIN'S HIGHLAND FARMS BED & BREAKFAST

70 East Road
Doylestown
☎ 215-340-1354
Moderate to Expensive

Stephen Sondheim, a local Bucks County boy whom Hammerstein coached in the rarefied art of writing for Broadway, and another local, James Michener, were among Hammerstein's many well-known guests.

Oscar Hammerstein and his wife lived in this 21-room stone-and-stucco manor home from 1941 to 1961. Within one year of moving to Highland Farms, Hammerstein was inspired to write his first in a string of American musicals, the classic *Oklahoma!* On the day the show opened on Broadway, Hammerstein (with several failures to his name) took a walk with his wife on a country road near Highland and said, "I don't know what to do if they don't like this. I don't know what to do because this is the only kind of show I can write." *Oklahoma!*, of course, ran for five years straight and transformed musical theater.

★ FAMOUS FACES

Oscar Hammerstein bought a farm in Doylestown in 1940 and wrote *Oh, What a Beautiful Mornin'* while sitting on his front porch.

Now a bed & breakfast, the 10-acre property features an in-ground pool, four-course breakfast and guest rooms named after Hammerstein's hit musicals: *Carousel*; *The King and I*; *Oklahoma!*; and *Show Boat*. Hammerstein memorabilia is scattered throughout.

★ FAMOUS FACES

Henry Fonda married Oscar and Dorothy Hammerstein's daughter, Susan Blanchard, under the grape arbor at the rear of the Highland Farms property.

THE DOYLESTOWN INN
18 West State Street
Doylestown
☎ 215-345-6610
www.doylestowninn.com
Moderate

After being closed for three years for renovations, The Doylestown Inn reopened in August 2001. Built in 1871 to house a hat shop and shoe store, this national landmark has served as a hotel since 1902.

The newly renovated hotel features a bakery and café on the first floor, professional and business offices on the second, and 11 guest rooms on the third. Owner Michael Welch, who purchased the hotel in 1998, originally planned to renovate all 20 of the inn's former rooms but, after the project dragged on for more than two years, announced he would forgo the rooms altogether. A compromise was struck between Welch and the Borough of Doylestown, whose council members desperately wanted a downtown place for visitors to stay. The result is pleasing. Rooms feature reproductions of antique furniture, private baths and whirlpool tubs.

Doylestown

Best Places to Eat

DINING PRICE SCALE

*Pricing includes one entrée, with
glass of wine and coffee.*

Inexpensive . . . . under $20
Moderate . . . . $20-$35
Expensive . . . . over $35

French

CAFE ARIELLE
100 South Main Street
☎ 215-345-5930
Moderate to Expensive

Housed in a restored 1800s livery stable, this romantic French bistro is well known for its duck and seafood entrées. Original artwork graces the walls; white linen cloths, candles and fresh flowers adorn the tables. The kitchen is open, and chef/owner Jacques Colmaire offers innovative seasonal menus.

Eclectic

BLACK WALNUT
80 West State Street
☎ 215-348-8244
Moderate to Expensive

Be sure to ask about Black Walnut chef Jack Gudin's demonstration and discussion cooking classes.

This homey but elegant restaurant features country dishes from regional American to Asian, Italian and Provençal French. Choose from modern, flavorful cuisine such as Brazilian lobster tails with shiitake mushrooms, or spring lamb chops with Moroccan spices. For dessert, try the signature Queen of Sheba – a warm Belgian chocolate soufflé cake. The wine list features small, artisanal vineyards.

Doylestown A to Z

Doylestown

Animal Hospitals

Animal Clinic-Doylestown, 1960 South Easton Road, ☎ 215-340-1838.

Doylestown Animal Medical Clinic, 802 North Easton Road, ☎ 215-345-7782.

New Britain Animal Clinic, 341 Butler Avenue, ☎ 215-340-0345.

Pheasant Run Animal Hospital, 12 Pheasant Road, ☎ 215-348-9099.

Rockhill Veterinary Associates, 341 Butler Avenue, ☎ 215-340-0345.

Banks

Commerce National Bank, 577 North Main Street, ☎ 215-489-3420.

First County Bank, 842 North Easton Road, ☎ 215-348-8620.

First National Bank & Trust Company, ☎ 215-340-0500.

Firstrust Bank, 288 South Main Street, ☎ 215-340-0069.

First Service Bank, 152 North Main Street, ☎ 215-230-4920.

First Union, 115 West Court Street, ☎ 215-345-4200.

First Union National Bank, 4259 West Swamp Road, ☎ 215-340-4705.

Harleysville National Bank, 500 Farm Lane, ☎ 215-230-5532.

Food Markets

Acme Markets, 480 North Main Street, ☎ 215-340-1341.

Acme Markets, 1745 South Easton Road, #6, ☎ 215-343-5520.

Clemens Market, 200 Town Center, New Britain, ☎ 215-345-0334.

Country Food Market, 203 West State Street, ☎ 215-348-8845.

Genuardi's Family Markets, 73 Old Dublin Pike, ☎ 215-345-1830.

Super Fresh Store, Route 611 & 313, ☎ 215-348-7844.

Hospital

Doylestown Hospital, 595 State Street, ☎ 215-345-2000.

Movie Theater

County Theater, 20 East State Street, ☎ 215-345-6789.

Newspapers

Doylestown Patriot, 350 South Main Street #10, ☎ 215-340-9811.

The Intelligencer, 333 North Broad Street, Doylestown, PA, ☎ 215-345-3000, www.intelligencer-record.com.

Pharmacies

Acme Markets, 480 North Main Street, ☎ 215-340-1341, and 1745 South Easton Road #6, ☎ 215-343-5520.

CVS Pharmacy, 4361 Routes 611 & 313, ☎ 215-348-7810.

Eckerd, 400 North Main Street, ☎ 215-345-1020; Route 611 & Almhouse, ☎ 215-343-4830; and 5176 Cold Spring Creamery Road, ☎ 215-489-5485.

Harris Pharmacy & Home Health, 511 East Street, ☎ 215-345-4800.

Rite Aid Pharmacies, Route 202, Town Center, New Britain, ☎ 215-340-5040.

Whitman's Pharmacy, 4950 York Road, Holicong, PA, ☎ 215-794-8850.

Post Offices

Doylestown, 8 Atkinson Drive, ☎ 215-348-8114.

New Britain, Route 202, ☎ 215-348-3399.

Religious Services

Church of Jesus Christ, Chapman & Ferry Road, ☎ 215-345-4430.

Covenant Presbyterian Church, 3434 Durham Road, ☎ 215-794-7909.

Doylestown Friends Meeting, 95 East Oakland Avenue, ☎ 215-348-2320.

Doylestown Mennonite Church, 590 North Broad Street, ☎ 215-345-6377.

Doylestown Presbyterian Church, 127 East Court Street, ☎ 215-348-3531.

Doylestown United Methodist, 320 East Swamp Road, ☎ 215-348-5224.

First Baptist Church, 311 West State Street, ☎ 215-348-5210.

First Church of Christ Scientist, 66 West State Street, ☎ 215-348-2150.

Main Street Baptist, 59 South Main Street, ☎ 215-348-8086.

Our Lady of Czestochowa Shrine, 654 Ferry Road, ☎ 215-345-0600.

Our Lady of Mount Carmel, 235 East State Street, ☎ 215-348-4190.

Peace Valley Church, 72 North Main Street, ☎ 215-230-7300.

Second Baptist Church, 1109 North Easton Road, ☎ 215-766-7650.

Wine & Spirits

Doylestown State Liquor Store, 132 Veterans Lane, ☎ 215-489-5202.

State Liquor Store, 19 West Court Street, Doylestown, ☎ 215-489-5207.

Doylestown

Princeton

But I found Princeton fine. A pipe as yet unsmoked. Young and fresh.

— Albert Einstein, 1921

Only a half-hour (or so) from the Delaware River in central New Jersey, Princeton is a definite must-see for any visitor to the Delaware River Valley. A long-time intellectual center, Princeton has been home to world-renowned scholars, scientists, writers and statesmen, including two US presidents.

> ## ※ HISTORIC TRIVIA
>
> Presidents **Woodrow Wilson** and **Grover Cleveland** both lived in Princeton.

History

Settled in the late 17th century, Princeton – just an hour from New York City – was named "Prince-Town" in honor of Prince William of Orange and Nassau. In 1756, the town became the home of the College of New Jersey (now Princeton University) with the entire college housed in Nassau Hall, then the largest academic building in the colonies.

During the Revolutionary War, the Battle of Princeton, fought on a nearby field in January 1777, was a decisive victory for General George Washington and his troops.

For a brief period – four months in 1783 – Princeton served as the nation's capital, with the Continental Congress convening in the University's Nassau Hall.

Princeton

NOT TO SCALE

© 2002 HUNTER PUBLISHING, INC.

1. Princeton Battlefield State Park
2. Institute for Advanced Study
3. Princeton's "Dinky" Station
4. McCarter Theatre
5. Princeton University Buildings
6. Bainbridge House
7. Palmer Square; Palmer House
8. Princeton Cemetery
9. Princeton Airport
10. Princeton Shopping Center
11. Main University Campus (see Princeton University map)

In 1930, the **Institute for Advanced Study** (see page 196) was founded in Princeton and was the first residential institute for scholars in the country. **Albert Einstein** served as one of its first professors.

★ TIP

New Jersey Transit's North-east Corridor train line runs between New York's Penn Station and Trenton, New Jersey. Passengers for Princeton University change at Princeton Junction to the "Dinky" train, which stops at Princeton Station.

The history of Princeton was shaped by the influx of immigrants from Ireland, Scotland, Germany, Eastern Europe and Italy at the turn of the 20th century. Today, Princeton is a dynamic cultural town. Its residents work in diverse fields, and there is a fast-growing Mexican community, but it still has a small, hometown feel. In addition to its world-renowned university, Princeton is widely celebrated for its arts, culture, architecture and shopping.

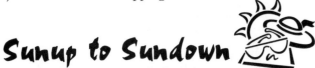

Sunup to Sundown

Walking Tours

The **Historical Society of Princeton** offers both guided and self-guided tours of Princeton. Their **Sunday Walking Tour** leaves every Sunday at 2 p.m. from Bainbridge House at 158 Nassau Street (see page 199). This leisurely guided tour takes two hours and covers 1.9 miles. Reservations are not necessary. Adults, $6; children six-12, $3; children under five free.

Artisans from Italy, Scotland and Ireland contributed to Princeton's rich architectural history.

The Society also offers two self-guided tours. The **Tour of Historic Princeton** takes walkers to historic sites within easy distance of the center of town, while **Small Town, Distinguished Architects** showcases Princeton buildings designed by some of the country's leading architects. These tours also begin at Bainbridge House. Call ☎ 609-921-6748 for tour information.

One-hour **Orange Key** tours of Princeton University are offered daily by student guides. Tours are by appointment and depart from the welcome desk at the Frist Campus Center on Washington Road (☎ 609-258-1766), Monday through Saturday at 10 a.m, 11 a.m., 1:30 p.m. and 3:30 p.m.; and Sundays at 1:30 p.m. and 3:30 p.m.

Historic Sites

Princeton University

First on the agenda for any trip to Princeton is a walk through the Princeton University campus. Ivy clings to elaborate stone buildings and black squirrels (unique to Princeton) dart about playfully. The University (formerly known as the College of New Jersey) moved to Princeton from Newark in 1756. Nassau Hall housed the entire college for nearly half a century. In 1896, when expanded program offerings brought the institution to university status, the College of New Jersey was officially renamed Princeton University in honor of its host community. Princeton has been fully coeducational since 1969, and during

Princeton University

© 2002 HUNTER PUBLISHING, INC.

1. Princeton's "Dinky" Station
2. McCarter Theatre
3. Institute for Advanced Study; Einstein House; Princeton Battlefield State Park
4. Drumthwacket
5. Palmer House
6. Palmer Square
7. Princeton Cemetery
8. Bainbridge House
9. Nassau Hall; McLean House
10. University Chapel; Dickinson Hall
11. Hamilton-Murray Theater
12. McCormick Hall
13. Prospect House & Gardens
14. Boat House

Princeton

its most recent academic year enrolled more than 6,000 students.

In touring the present-day campus, several buildings are of special note, the first being its chapel.

PRINCETON UNIVERSITY CHAPEL
Built between 1925 and 1928, the Princeton University Chapel is modeled after the chapel of King's College, Cambridge; it seats more than 2,000 people on pews made from army-surplus wood originally intended for Civil War gun carriages. The chancel's paneling was carved in England from Sherwood Forest oak trees; the exterior is of Pennsylvania sandstone with Indian limestone trim. The Chapel, elaborate and gothic in architectural style, replaces the smaller Marquand Chapel, built in 1881. Nondenominational services are held each week. Hours during the academic year are Monday through Friday, 8 a.m. to 11 p.m.; Saturday, 7:30 a.m. to 6:30 p.m.; and Sunday, 7 a.m. to 11 p.m. Summer hours are Monday through Saturday, 7:30 a.m. to 4:15 p.m. and Sunday, 7 a.m. to 3:30 p.m.; ☎ 609-258-3048.

✖ HISTORIC TRIVIA

Princeton University's Marquand Chapel was lost to fire in 1920, after a group of University students torched a nearby building, Dickinson Hall, which contained a giant exam hall on its roof. The fire skipped across to the roof of the Marquand, destroying the chapel completely.

The Treaty of Paris, formally ending the American Revolution, was signed in Princeton's Nassau Hall.

NASSAU HALL
At one time, Nassau Hall housed the entire University. Today, the regal building is home to the offices of the University's president and administrative staff. The building survived occupation by both British and Colonial troops during the Revolutionary

War – and two fires – and for a short time (four months in 1783) served as the nation's capitol. Today, portraits of Princeton's founders, past presidents and famous alumni are displayed in the Hall. Also included are hand portraits of George II and William III.

PROSPECT HOUSE & GARDENS

This Italianate-style mansion is one of the few University buildings not originally a part of the campus. It was built as a home in 1849, and was named for its commanding views of the surrounding countryside. The house was presented to Princeton University in 1878, and University president James McCosh thought the house was "the finest in the world for a college president" and that "its grounds were like Eden."

Princeton University has educated two US presidents (Woodrow Wilson and Grover Cleveland), hundreds of US and state legislators, and 44 governors.

As the campus enlarged, however, students began taking shortcuts across the lawns and gardens, depriving the property of its "Eden-like" qualities. After a rampaging football crowd trespassed across the lawn in 1904, Woodrow Wilson (president of the University at the time) erected an iron fence, enclosing five acres of the grounds. Shortly thereafter, his wife laid the groundwork for the flower garden, which remains spectacular to this day. Prospect House & Gardens is a popular wedding spot for alumni and employees of Princeton University. The house itself is now a private club, but the gardens are open to the public daily, until dusk; admission is free.

Princeton

INSTITUTE FOR ADVANCED STUDY

Princeton's renowned Institute for Advanced Study was founded in 1930 by educator **Abraham Flexner**, who recruited noted mathematicians from Princeton University to join the Institute. In 1932, Albert Einstein accepted a faculty position at the Institute, where he continued his research until his death in 1955. Flexner envisioned " ... a haven where scholars and scientists may regard the world and its phenomena as their laboratory without being carried off in the maelstrom of the immediate."

Visitors are welcome to use the Institute's 500-acre nature reserve for hiking, running, cross-country skiing and birdwatching. There is a public parking area at Battlefield Park on Mercer Street, and trail maps are available at the reception desk in Fuld Hall (open Monday through Friday, from 9 a.m. to 5 p.m.). The Institute for Advanced Study, Einstein Drive, ☎ 609-734-8000.

EINSTEIN HOUSE

Albert Einstein, whose theory of relativity made him a worldwide celebrity, lived at 112 Mercer Street in Princeton from 1936 until his death in 1955. Einstein's daughter, Margot, and his personal secretary, Helen Dukas, remained in the house until their deaths in 1986 and 1982, respectively. At Einstein's request, the house has never been turned into a museum or public shrine. Owned by the **Institute for Advanced Study**, the house is presently a private residence, but that doesn't stop curiosity seekers from gawking at it.

Princeton Architecture

Aside from the University, the town of Princeton offers an astounding collection of architectural treasures. These are among the notable examples.

BAINBRIDGE HOUSE

Currently the headquarters of the Historical Society of Princeton, this Georgian building is one of the few remaining 18th-century houses in Princeton Borough. Almost all of the 1766 structure remains, including original paneled walls and staircase. The house was built by **Job Stockton**, a wealthy tanner and descendent of one of the earliest Princeton settlers. It remained in the Stockton family for more than 100 years. In the late 19th century, Bainbridge House served as a boarding house for families and Princeton University students. It became the home of the Historical Society in 1967. Open Tuesday-Sunday, noon to 4 p.m.; weekends only in January and February. 158 Nassau Street, ☎ 609-921-6748.

Princeton

DRUMTHWACKET

Nationally known architects Benjamin Latrobe, Ralph Adams Cram, Robert Venturi, Michael Graves, and the firm of McKim, Mead & White have all designed buildings in Princeton.

Located just south of downtown, Drumthwacket is the official residence of the Governor of New Jersey. The mansion was built in 1835 by **Charles Olden**, a Civil War-era governor, and was enlarged in 1895. The house is operated by the Drumthwacket Foundation and is open for tours on Wednesdays, from noon to 2 p.m. 354 Stockton Street (Route 206), ☎ 609-683-0057.

✕ HISTORIC TRIVIA

Grover Cleveland and his wife settled in Princeton after his second presidential term ended in 1897. The Clevelands purchased a Georgian Revival house at 15 Hodge Road. The home became a gathering place for undergraduates, especially after athletic or debating triumphs. Grover Cleveland died in 1908 and is buried in Princeton Cemetery.

PRINCETON CEMETERY

Princeton Cemetery, the resting place of many prominent figures in American history, has still-legible graves dating back to 1760, including those of **Aaron Burr**, **Grover Cleveland**, and Cleveland's daughter **Ruth** of Baby Ruth candy bar fame. Maps are stored in the little box just inside the gate; guided tours of the cemetery are available by appointment. The cemetery is at the intersection of Witherspoon and Wiggins streets, and is open daily, from dawn to dusk; ☎ 609-924-1369.

Recreation

Biking

With traffic heavy in downtown Princeton, you may prefer to get around by bike rather than by car. **Jay's Cycles**, 249 Nassau Street (☎ 609-924-7233), rents bikes, as does **Kopps Cycle**, 38 Spring Street (☎ 609-924-1052).

Flightseeing Rides

Princeton Airport, located in Rocky Hill just three miles north of Princeton on Route 206, offers one-hour flightseeing rides ($120 per hour for three adults), as well as one-hour introductory flight lessons ($109 per person). Reservations are necessary; ☎ 609-921-3100.

Lake Carnegie

Princeton's Lake Carnegie was the gift of Scottish-American steelmaker **Andrew Carnegie** to Princeton University President Woodrow Wilson in 1906. The man-made lake, located along the southern edge of the University's main campus, was intended to promote clean, wholesome sports, such as rowing, at the University, and to provide the entire community with a place to enjoy recreational activities like fishing, sailing and ice skating. The lake is 3.5 miles long and is bordered by the Delaware & Raritan Ca-

Lake Carnegie was the first man-made lake built in the United States specifically for collegiate rowing.

nal. It was added to the National Register of Historic places in 1991 as a conservation measure.

Bring a picnic and watch University rowers. During summer months, small canoes may be rented at posts along the lake.

Spas

The interest in spa services is growing, and Princeton offers two excellent choices.

Metropolis was recently named "Best Day Spa" by readers of the *Princeton Packet*. Facials are fabulous, particularly the oxygenating facial. Body treatments include a Body Glo (using Dead Sea salts or honey, almond and oatmeal), as well as pregnancy and aromatherapy massages. One-on-one makeup lessons are popular, especially the Teen's First package. 310 Harrison Street, Princeton Shopping Center; ☎ 609-683-8388.

The Spa at Doral Forrestal offers more in-depth treatments, including Reiki, shiatsu and reflexology, along with European facials and exfoliating treatments. Yoga and meditation classes are available. This spa has all of the amenities, such as men's and women's locker rooms, a sauna, steam rooms, showers and special relaxation lounges. Appointments are necessary. 100 College Road East; ☎ 609-897-7520, www.forrestalspa.com.

Arts & Theater

Performing Arts

The McCarter Theatre

Built as a permanent home for the Princeton University **Triangle Club**, the **McCarter Theatre Center for Performing Arts** has a rich history of artists who have graced its stage. The theater first opened its doors in 1930 with a special performance of the 40th annual Triangle show, *The Golden Dog*. University sophomore **James Stewart** was in the chorus.

Every summer, the Opera Festival of New Jersey holds a gala event at the McCarter Theatre; ☎ 609-258-ARTS (2787).

During the 1930s, the McCarter gained popularity as a pre-Broadway showcase due to its seating capacity, its 40-foot proscenium stage and its short distance from New York City.

In the post-World War II years, Broadway producers cut costs by having extended preview periods in New York City rather than out-of-town tryouts. As the number of touring Broadway shows declined, the McCarter could no longer be self-supporting; in 1950, Princeton University and the Triangle Club agreed that the University would take title to the building and assume responsibility for its operating costs. Noted director Milton Lyon was hired in 1960 and, under his direction, the McCarter Theatre became a "producing" rather than "booking" theater.

Princeton

★ FAMOUS FACES

Thornton Wilder's *Our Town* made its world premiere at the McCarter Theatre, as did **George S. Kaufman** and **Moss Hart's** *You Can't Take It With You*; **James Thurber** and **Elliot Nugent's** *The Male Animal* (starring Gene Tierney); **Philip Barry's** *Without Love* (starring Katherine Hepburn) and **William Inge's** *Bus Stop* (starring Kim Stanley and Elaine Stritch).

Now under the leadership of artistic director Emily Mann and director Jeffrey Woodward, the McCarter Theatre is renowned for fostering new works and presenting innovative interpretations of classic dramatic literature.

In 1994, the McCarter was awarded a Tony Award for Outstanding Regional Theatre. In 1995, Ms. Mann wrote and directed the world premiere of *Having Our Say* on the McCarter stage before it enjoyed a Broadway run (where it garnered three Tony nominations), a national tour, a South African production, and culminated in a Peabody Award-winning television movie.

In 1999, the McCarter was again represented on Broadway with its production of *Electra*. In addition to regular staged productions, the McCarter hosts one-night-only special events. Book tickets ahead of time. Box office, 91 University Place, ☎ 888-ARTS-WEB (278-7932), www.mccarter.org.

Theatre Intime

Theatre Intime takes its name from the French word for "intimate." And intimate is the best way to describe the charming, stone, 200-seat **Hamilton-Murray Theater** at Princeton University where the college troupe performs. The acting troupe began in 1920, when a group of students staged their first play in a college dormitory room. The next year they moved to Murray Hall, which was being used as a chapel. Since those humble beginnings, the student group has tackled everything from Greek tragedy to Shakespeare. Students act, direct, fund-raise and administer, receiving no support from the University. Landmark productions have included *Amadeus*, *Noises Off*, *Rosencrantz and Guildenstern are Dead*, and *Arcadia*. Hamilton-Murray Theater, Princeton University Campus, ☎ 609-258-4950, www.theatre-intime.org.

During World War II, Princeton's Murray Theater was given over to Navy lecturers and Intime's activities were suspended.

The American Boy Choir

♪♪♫ Based in Princeton, the choir tours cities across the United States and has performed on numerous radio, TV and movie soundtracks with such notables as the New York Pops, the New York Philharmonic Orchestra and the Vienna Philharmonic. The Boy Choir hosts an annual holiday concert at Princeton's Richardson Auditorium. If you are in town in December, be sure to check local listings for scheduled performances.

Princeton

Uniquely Princeton

Princeton may seem an unlikely destination for an agricultural population from a remote southern Mexican town, but residents of Putla, Mexico are flocking here.

"People follow the crowd," reports Felipe Cruz, owner of Princeton's Taste of Mexico restaurant. "People come here directly from Mexico because they have people they know here and they have relatives. Half of my hometown now lives here."

Princeton's Mexican immigration actually began in the 1970s when two brothers came to the United States in search of work – and ultimately a better life. They were hired by a Nicaraguan woman, Ruth Alegria, who owned a Mexican restaurant in New York City. When Ms. Alegria decided to open a second place in Princeton, she persuaded the brothers (Christian and Gildardo Guzman) to come with her. Soon, wives, girlfriends, sons and nephews were also on their way to Princeton. Many of the former Putlecan residents have opened businesses in Princeton's Witherspoon neighborhood. A walk down Witherspoon Street (from Nassau Street toward the hospital) reveals tiny Mexican grocery stores and small mom-and-pop Mexican restaurants.

Fine Arts

The Art Museum

Look for Picasso's large sculpture, *Head of a Woman*, marking this small but treasure-filled fine-arts museum located in **McCormick Hall**, at the center of the Princeton campus. Permanent collections range from ancient to contemporary art, with concentrations in the Mediterranean regions, Western Europe, China, the United States and Latin America. There's also an outstanding collection of Greek and Roman antiquities, including ceramics, marbles and bronzes, and Roman mosaics from Princeton University's excavations in Antioch. Special exhibits are also featured. Highlight tours of the museum are held Saturdays at 2 p.m.; children's talks are given Saturdays at 11 a.m. McCormick Hall, ☎ 609-258-3788, http://webware.princeton.edu/artmus.

Lost and Found Gallery

This unusual gallery – featuring recycled junk – opened in November of 2001, and there's nothing quite like it in Princeton or elsewhere. All of the items in the store are handcrafted by national and international artists. There are lunchboxes made from olive-oil cans, baskets made from videotape and film, mirrors framed in yardsticks and step stools created from antique signs. No two items are the same; all are limited editions. Even if you don't buy, it's worth taking a look to see how one man's junk can artistically become another man's treasure. Lost and Found is open Tuesday through Thursday, 10:30 a.m. to 5:30 p.m.; Friday until 7 p.m.; Saturday until 6 p.m.; and Sunday, 11 a.m. to 4:30 p.m.; closed Mondays. 20 Nassau Street, ☎ 609-497-9499.

Princeton

FAMOUS FACES

Princeton resident and famed children's book illustrator **Gennady Spirin** was born in the small town of Orekhovo-Zuyevo near Moscow. He came to Princeton more than a decade ago; since then, his elaborate and intricately detailed illustrations have earned critical praise and numerous awards. Spirin's exquisitely rendered illustrations in vivid watercolors have appeared in more than 30 books, including those selected by *The New York Times* as "Best Illustrated Books of the Year" (*The Fool and the Fish*; *Gulliver's Adventures in Lilliput, Kashtanka*, and *The Sea King's Daughter*).

 # Shop Till You Drop

Shopping in Princeton is priceless – literally. From Ann Taylor to Laura Ashley, Talbots and Waverly, the upscale possibilities of shopping this town's tiny boutiques are endless. Most of the best shopping is along **Nassau Street** and around **Palmer Square**. The square was designed by Edgar Palmer, heir to the New Jersey Zinc Company fortune, in 1929; the Depression slowed Palmer's project to a start date of 1936, and the square was not completed until the 1980s when stores and townhouses were finally added on the north and east sides.

Most stores in Princeton are open Monday through Wednesday, 10 a.m. to 6 p.m.; Thursday and Friday, 10 a.m. to 9 p.m.; Saturday, 10 a.m. to 6 p.m.; and

Sunday, noon to 5 p.m. Highlights of a shopping trip in Princeton should include the following stores.

Clothing

ANN TAYLOR
This upscale specialty store, located in the heart of Palmer Square, is well known for its sophisticated, fashionable and classic clothing. 17 Palmer Square, ☎ 609-924-8335.

APRIL CORNELL
This tiny boutique showcases the unique designs of April Cornell via women's and children's clothing, as well as bed and table linens. 51 Palmer Square, ☎ 609-924-3559.

LANDAU'S
Family-run since 1955, Landau's imports pure European woolens. Jackets and sweaters are especially nice here. At Christmas time, an Icelandic fisherman sells fresh-smoked salmon. 102 Nassau Street, ☎ 609-924-3494.

ZOE'S
Located on Palmer Square, this artsy boutique (albeit pricey) is a paradise for funky dresses, jeans, sweaters, shoes, purses and outrageous cosmetics. Clothing is unique and unusual, and their sales yield significant bargains. Palmer Square, ☎ 609-497-0704.

Princeton

THE EINSTEIN EXHIBIT

Landau's owner, Robert Landau, has the only Einstein exhibit in the world. Landau, dismayed by the absence of an Einstein commemoration in Princeton, started his own Einstein exhibit in one corner of his store. The collection began with one picture held in the Landau family archives, then grew after other Princetonians donated Einstein memorabilia.

Home Décor

MATTEO & COMPANY
This home furnishings specialty store features fine linens, upholstered furniture, infant bedding, bath products and antiques. Palmer Square, ☎ 609-430-8205.

ETC. COMPANY
Also on Palmer Square, Etc. Company offers great furniture as well as home accessories and bath products. Palmer Square, ☎ 609-279-9093.

Gifts & Accessories

BOWHE & PEARE
This specialty store has great housewares and gifts and, at Christmas time, nativities hand-selected from countries around the world. 27 Palmer Square, ☎ 609-924-2086.

THE SALTY DOG

Flags of many nations surround the front door of this eclectic store, selling wares from around the world. Here, you'll find Buddha statues, carvings from Africa, handmade jewelry, and other unique items from Tibet, Thailand, and virtually every corner of the globe. 4 Spring Street, ☎ 609-924-0455.

MICAWBER BOOKS

Located downtown on Nassau Street, Micawber Books is one of the few remaining independent bookstores in the area. The selection is huge, with lots of events such as author readings and book signings. They have a great selection of children's books as well. Open Monday through Saturday, 9 a.m. to 8 p.m.; Sunday, 11 a.m. to 5 p.m. 110-114 Nassau Street, ☎ 609-921-8454.

After Dark

Concerts & Cultural Events

Princeton

There is almost always a concert of some sort going on in Princeton, whether it be downtown or at the University. One of the best cultural guides to the area is a free newspaper called *US1*, found in stores and newspaper boxes around town; the paper highlights cultural activities week by week.

Bars, Clubs & Dancing

Princeton has a small bar scene, with several clubs featuring live music on a regular basis.

TRIUMPH BREWING COMPANY
Both a restaurant and a pub, Triumph offers one of Princeton's only dance spaces (albeit a small one). The real draw isn't the live music on Friday and Saturday nights, but the beer – Triumph operates a brewery, and has its own beers on tap. 138 Nassau Street, ☎ 609-924-7857.

YANKEE DOODLE TAP ROOM
Located in the historic Nassau Inn, the Yankee Doodle Tap Room features a late-night bar menu and live jazz on weekends. 10 Palmer Square, ☎ 609-921-7500.

IVY INN
Many contend that this no-frills bar is "the college bar that Princeton does not have." A lone picture of former New Jersey Senator and Princeton University basketball player Bill Bradley on the wall is perfect for toasting, and drinks hover around $2. 248 Nassau Street, ☎ 609-921-8555.

BROADWAY BALLROOM
This club in downtown Princeton hosts occasional Saturday-night dance parties. Swing, salsa and other Latin dances are featured. No need to worry if you're rusty, as lessons are included, but partners usually aren't, so bring one. Dance parties are held September through June; call ahead for cost and

time as there is no set schedule. 4-6 Hulfish Street, ☎ 609-924-8970.

Best Places to Stay

As a University town, the Princeton area offers a wide range of accommodations from deluxe Hyatts and Marriotts to smaller chain hotels. All such accommodations are located out of town on US-1. In town, Princeton is home to two historic inns.

ACCOMMODATIONS PRICE SCALE
Price scale is based on a standard room for two persons, per night.
Inexpensive . . . . under $100
Moderate . . . . $100-$200
Expensive . . . . $201-$300
Deluxe . . . . more than $300

THE PEACOCK INN
20 Bayard Lane
☎ 609-921-0050
Moderate

Freshly painted in bold, vibrant colors, Princeton's proud Peacock Inn is one of the town's most historic buildings. On the tax rolls since 1775, the inn was moved from the Princeton University campus to its present location during the 1800s. The private home became an inn in 1912 and has welcomed a host of illustrious guests, including **Bertrand Russell**, **Albert Einstein** and **F. Scott Fitzgerald**.

The gambrel-roofed inn, with its huge front porch, offers 17 guest rooms, an elegant French restaurant and a bar. Rooms vary in color scheme and décor, featuring French, Early American and English antiques and reproductions. There is a peacock theme, of course; the showy bird appears on mantels, bedside lamps and screens. The owners even have six live peacocks (not on the premises).

The Peacock Inn is Princeton's only bed & breakfast and it books early, especially in spring and fall when alums and parents fill the rooms.

☞ **DID YOU KNOW?**

In 1933, Albert Einstein accepted a position at the newly created Institute for Advanced Study. He, along with his wife, Elsa, and personal secretary, Helen Dukas, spent 10 days at the Peacock Inn. Elsa looked for a suitable house, while Albert dodged reporters.

NASSAU INN
10 Palmer Square
☎ 609-921-7500
www.nassauinn.com
Expensive to Deluxe

A better location is hard to find. Built in 1756, Princeton's classic Nassau Inn sits right in the center of Palmer Square. Princeton University, shopping and restaurants are all within easy walking distance. The inn has 203 rooms, including suites named for Princeton luminaries like actor **Christopher Reeve**, **Albert Einstein**, and **Norman Rockwell** (who painted the mural inside the inn's Yankee Doodle Tap Room). All of the inn's rooms have been recently renovated and feature reproductions of Colonial-era pieces and turndown service with homemade cookies.

PRINCETON MARRIOTT
201 Village Boulevard
Princeton Forrestal Village
☎ 609-452-7900
Moderate to Expensive

This six-floor, 294-room hotel is, itself, a destination. Located in the middle of Princeton's Forrestal Village, an enclave of more than 40 factory outlet stores about five miles from downtown Princeton, the hotel has all the amenities: two restaurants (Allies American Grille and Mikado Japanese Steakhouse), an indoor/outdoor pool, health club, sauna, jogging paths and tennis.

HYATT REGENCY PRINCETON
102 Carnegie Center
☎ 609-987-1234
Moderate to Expensive

This four-story hotel, with open atriums, waterfalls and greenery, opened in the 1980s as the area's first deluxe hotel. It continues to accommodate business travelers and out-of-town guests. The hotel features 348 rooms, with 14 suites. Amenities include an indoor heated pool, fitness center, jogging path and saunas. For night owls, there is a wine bar, "By The Glass," and a comedy club that features live comedians on Wednesday, Thursday, Friday and Saturday

Princeton

A piano player serenades in the Hyatt Regency's By The Glass wine bar on Friday and Saturday nights, and in the Crystal Garden Restaurant during Sunday brunch.

nights. The hotel's Crystal Garden Restaurant is famous for its Sunday brunch, served 11:30 a.m. to 2:30 p.m.

> ⭐ **TIP**
>
> The Princeton Airporter makes daily runs from the Nassau Inn, Princeton Marriott Forrestal Village, and Doral Forrestal Hotel & Spa to JFK International Airport ($38 one way) and Newark International Airport ($23 one way). Check the schedule at ☎ 800-385-4000; www.goairporter.com.

DORAL FORRESTAL HOTEL & SPA

100 College Road East
Princeton
☎ 609-452-7800
www.doralforrestal.com
Inexpensive to Expensive

Located near Forrestal Village shopping area, Doral Forrestal Hotel features 290 rooms, each decorated in the style of the turn-of-the-century California Arts & Crafts movement. Two restaurants, a bar (eight beers on tap) and club room (for playing cards, watching sports and smoking cigars) provide plenty to do when taking a break from downtown. There is also a pool, tennis courts, bicycles, sauna, fitness center and full-service spa (see page 200).

★ FAMOUS FACES

The "Wall of Fame" in the Nassau Inn's Yankee Doodle Tap Room showcases well-known Princeton University graduates, including former senator Bill Bradley, Brooke Shields, and Charlie Gibson.

Best Places to Eat

"Intellectually rich… gastronomically deprived" has long been Princeton's well-deserved reputation. Fortunately, Princeton's dining experience is changing. Following are a few of the town's culinary standouts.

DINING PRICE SCALE
Pricing includes one entrée, with glass of wine and coffee.
Inexpensive . . . . under $20
Moderate . . . . $20-$35
Expensive . . . . over $35

Princeton

Casual Eateries

PJ's PANCAKES
154 Nassau Street
☎ 609-924-1353
www.pancakes.com
Inexpensive

Located in the center of town, PJ's Pancakes has been a Princeton icon for more than 35 years. The restaurant is heavily patronized by Princeton University students and alumni who carve their names into the wooden table tops. Pancakes, all shapes, sizes and flavors, dominate the menu, but there are also the usual burgers and fries, soups and desserts. Be prepared to wait for a table on Sunday mornings. PJ's is open Sunday through Thursday, 7 a.m. to 10 p.m.; Friday and Saturday, 7 a.m. to midnight.

★ CULINARY SECRET

Princeton has its own brewery – located at **Triumph Brew Pub**, 38 Nassau Street, ☎ 609-924-7855.

CHUCK'S SPRING STREET CAFE
16 Spring Street
☎ 609-921-0027
Cash only
Inexpensive

Hot-and-spicy Buffalo wings are the specialty of this small, cafeteria-style eatery. Located on a side street, Chuck's is easy to miss, but once you've been here, you'll instinctively find your way back. There are probably better Buffalo wings somewhere (in Buffalo, perhaps), but it's hard to imagine. Wings are sold in quantities of 14 to 100 for different set prices. There are other offerings on the menu – sandwiches, salads, soups and fries – but Buffalo wings are definitely the house specialty.

OLIVES
22 Witherspoon Street
☎ 609-921-1569
Inexpensive

Open daily, this gourmet bakery and deli is jam-packed at lunch hour as locals pick up food to take back to the office, or for picnics on the green at Palmer Square. Try the Greek specialties, such as spinach pie, stuffed grape leaves and baklava. Open Monday through Saturday, 7 a.m. to 8 p.m.; Sunday, 9 a.m. to 5 p.m.

★ CULINARY SECRET

Princeton has seen a surge of cozy coffee shops in recent years. For great java, try **Small World Coffee's** house blend, called Grumpy Monkey. 14 Witherspoon Street, ☎ 609-497-1170.

CONTE'S PIZZA
339 Witherspoon Street
☎ 609-921-8041
Inexpensive

The original Princeton pizza joint, this long-time favorite is a bare-bones, pizza-and-beer, watch-the-game-while-you-eat kind of place. Locals congregate here after softball and other sporting events and

Princeton

there's typically a long wait. Thin crust is the defining ingredient for the pizza. Monday through Friday, 4 to 11 p.m.; Saturday, 4:30 to 11:30 p.m.

★ CULINARY SECRET

Panera Bread serves hearty soups and chowders in sourdough bowls. Open daily, 136 Nassau Street, ☎ 609-683-5222.

Eclectic

FERRY HOUSE
32 Witherspoon Street
☎ 609-924-2488
BYOB
Moderate to Expensive

If you're planning to visit Ferry House on a Saturday night, call early in the week. If you don't, chances are the only slots left will be for very early or very late in the evening.

Chef **Bobby Triggs** moved his popular restaurant from Lambertville to Princeton several years ago, where he has maintained a loyal following. The décor is warm, with an eclectic mix of paintings that range from European landscapes to contemporary designs.

The menu changes bimonthly and is always a surprise. Rack of lamb and tuna are hailed as Mr. Triggs' specialties, and raw oysters are served nightly. Desserts do not disappoint. The Ferry House makes its own ice creams and sorbets, and its homemade crème brûlée is exceptional. Ferry House is open for lunch, Monday through Friday, 11:30 a.m. to 2:30 p.m.; and dinner, Monday through Saturday, 5 to 10 p.m.; and Sunday, 4 to 9 p.m.

British

SALLY LUNN'S RESTAURANT & TEA ROOM
164 Nassau Street
☎ 609-430-1071
Inexpensive

Step into a Jane Austen novel with this quintessentially English establishment, which serves high tea and British favorites such as shepherd's pie and Devonshire cheesecake. Décor is Victorian, complete with servers in period dress. Tables are covered in white crocheted tablecloths; walls are decorated with china plates, garlands and dried roses. Open Tuesday through Sunday, 10:30 a.m. to 5:30 p.m.; closed Mondays.

★ CULINARY SECRET

Thomas Sweet? Halo Pub? There is a growing (and unsolved) debate over which Princeton ice cream is better. Try them both for yourself! **Thomas Sweet**, 179 Nassau Street, ☎ 609-924-1353; **Halo Pub**, 9 Hulfish Street, ☎ 609-921-1710. Expect long lines at both.

Princeton

Italian

TERESA'S CAFE ITALIANO
19-23 Palmer Square East
☎ 609-921-1974
Moderate to Expensive

Whether for lunch, dinner or a late-night snack, there is always a wait at this popular eatery on Palmer Square. Start by dipping bread (tomato and basil is excellent) in olive oil, then move on to fresh salads and well-made pasta dishes, ending with a chocolate pizza. My daughter discovered this decadent dessert, which features a light pizza crust drizzled in chocolate-hazelnut sauce, and the delicacy has since replaced birthday cakes in our house. Open Monday through Saturday, 11 a.m. to 11 p.m.; Sunday, noon to 10 p.m. Expect a long wait; reservations are not accepted.

Mediterranean

MEDITERRA
29 Hulfish Street
☎ 609-252-9680
Moderate

Just behind Palmer Square, Mediterra is a captivating addition to the expanding Princeton restaurant scene. In summer dining is alfresco, spilling out toward an attractive piazza with a bubbling fountain.

As its name suggests, Mediterra features Mediterranean cuisine with starters like sun-dried tomato hummus (puréed chickpeas) accompanied by Parmesan crostini; and entrées of shrimp and Moroccan crab cake and grilled marinated lamb kebobs. Sunday through Thursday, 11:30 a.m. to 11 p.m.; Friday and Satuday, 11:30 a.m. to midnight.

Mexican

TORTUGA'S MEXICAN VILLAGE
44 Leigh Avenue
☎ 609-924-5143
BYOB; no credit cards
Inexpensive

Another always crowded hotspot, this authentic Mexican restaurant was named the third best Mexican restaurant in New Jersey by Zagat. Just two brightly painted rooms, Tortuga's is frequented mostly by locals, who come for the homemade salsa and chips, seafood enchiladas, chile rellenos, pollo mole and fajitas. Open for lunch, Monday through Friday, 11:30 a.m. to 2 p.m.; and dinner, daily, from 5:30 p.m.

EL SABOR MEXICANO
(Taste of Mexico)
301 North Harrison Street
☎ 609-252-1575
BYOB
Inexpensive

The mixed-in-front-of-you guacamole alone is reason to come. But the rest of the menu is worthy of exploration, too, and owner Felipe Cruz is about the friendliest host imaginable. Cruz, who hails from a small Mexican town near Putla, serves up authentic regional dishes and *jarritos* (Mexican soft drinks).

Princeton

> ★ **CULINARY SECRET**
>
> Princeton's **Bon Appétit**, an up-scale market and deli founded and still run by a Belgian family, carries more than 250 varieties of cheese. Open daily at 301 North Harrison Street, Princeton Shopping Center, ☎ 609-924-7755.

Princeton A to Z

Animal Hospital

Carnegie Cat Clinic, 726 Alexander Road, Princeton, ☎ 609-520-2000.

Harlingen Veterinary Clinic, 10 Sunset Road, Belle Mead, NJ, ☎ 908-359-2000.

Lawrence Hospital for Animals, 3975 Princeton Pike, Princeton, ☎ 609-924-2293.

Bank

First Union National Bank, 194 Nassau Street, ☎ 609-921-6000.

Food Markets

La Mexicanas, 150 Witherspoon Street, ☎ 609-279-9404.

McCaffrey's Princeton Market, 301 North Harrison Street, ☎ 609-683-1600.

Wegmans Food Markets, 240 Nassau Park Boulevard, ☎ 609-919-9300.

Wild Oats Community Market, 255 Nassau Street, ☎ 609-924-4993.

Hospital

Medical Center at Princeton, 253 Witherspoon Street, ☎ 609-497-4000.

Movie Theaters

Princeton Garden Theaters, 160 Nassau Street, ☎ 609-683-7595.

UA Movies at Market Fair, 3535 US Highway 1, ☎ 609-520-8700.

UA Theatre Circuit, US Highway 1 & Meadow Road, ☎ 609-520-8822.

Newspapers

Princeton Packet, 300 Witherspoon Street, ☎ 609-924-3244.

Town Topics, 4 Mercer Street, ☎ 609-924-2200.

US1, 12 Roszel Road, ☎ 609-452-0038.

Princeton

Pharmacies

CVS Pharmacy, 172 Nassau Street, ☎ 609-683-1391.

Eckerd, 301 North Harrison Street, ☎ 609-924-6125.

Forer Pharmacy, 160 Witherspoon Street, ☎ 609-921-7287.

Princeton Pharmacy, 36 University Place, ☎ 609-924-4545.

Post Offices

Princeton, 20 Palmer Square, ☎ 609-921-9563, and 213 Carnegie Center, ☎ 609-452-9044.

Religious Services

Aquinas Institute, 65 Stockton Street, ☎ 609-924-1820.

Bunker Hill Luthern Church, 235 Bunker Hill Road, ☎ 908-359-6302.

Episcopal Church at Princeton, 53 University Place, ☎ 609-252-9469.

First Baptist Church, John & Paul Robeson Place, ☎ 609-924-0877.

First Church of Christ Science, 16 Bayard Lane, ☎ 609-924-5801.

Lutheran Church of the Messiah, 407 Nassau Street, ☎ 609-924-3642.

Nassau Presbyterian Church, 61 Nassau Street, ☎ 609-924-0103.

Princeton Friends, 470 Quaker Road, ☎ 609-924-5674.

Princeton United Methodist Church, 160 Nassau Street, ☎ 609-924-2613.

Wine & Spirits

Claridge Wine & Liquor Company, 301 North Harrison Street, #16, ☎ 609-924-5700.

Community Liquors, 23 Witherspoon Street, ☎ 609-924-0750.

Nassau Liquors Grape & Grain, 264 Nassau Street, ☎ 609-924-0031.

Princeton Wine & Liquor, 174 Nassau Street, ☎ 609-924-0279.

Varsity Liquors, 234 Nassau Street, ☎ 609-924-0836.

Princeton

Index